METAVERSE INVESTING

BUSINESS GUIDE

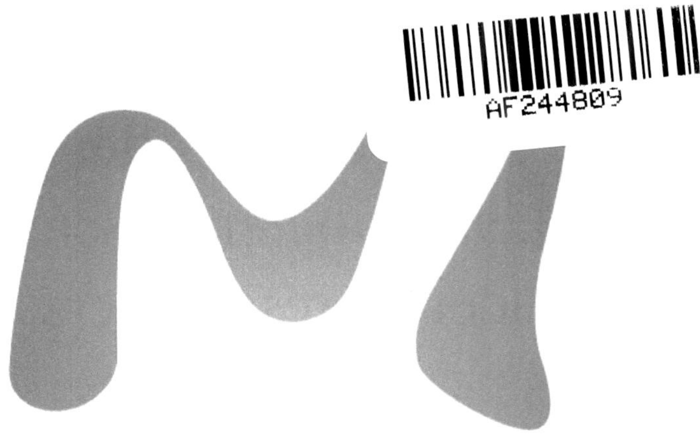

The Meta-Verse

ABOUT THE AUTHOR

The Meta-Verse

The Meta-Verse are researchers Based in London, England.

The Meta-Verse is a collective; we work with the most senior academic researchers.

We are in the changing lives business.

Want Future Book Releases?

Email us at:

<u>mindsetmastership@gmail.com</u>

Find us on Instagram!

@MindsetMastership

MASTERSHIP BOOKS

UK | USA | Canada | Ireland | Australia

India | New Zealand | South Africa | China

Mastership Books is part of the United Arts Publishing House group of companies based in London, England, UK.

First published by Mastership Books (London, UK), 2021

I S B N: 978-1-915002-09-9

Text Copyright © United Arts Publishing

Cover design by Rich © United Arts Publishing (UK)

Text and internal design by Rich © United Arts Publishing (UK)

Image credits reserved.

Colour separation by Spitting Image Design Studio

Printed and bound in Great Britain

National Publications Association of Britain

London, England, United Kingdom.

Paper design UAP

ISBN: 978-1-915002-09-9 (paperback)

A723.5

Title: **Metaverse Investing Business**

Design, Bound & Printed:

London, England,

Great Britain.

THE METAVERSE BUSINESS

"If you really want to invest in something today, start investing in NFTs, Metaverse and Domains, these hidden treasure and going mainstream"

CONTENTS

0

FUNDAMENTALS OF
THE METAVERSE

The metaverse is a collection of virtual environments where you may collaborate and create with individuals who are not physically there with you. You will be able to engage with your friends, work, play, explore, shop, and create, among other things. Metaverse is not about putting in more time online; it is about making the time you put in more worthwhile. Fortunately for businesses, the metaverse is not a single product that a single company can develop. The metaverse, similar to the internet, exists whether or not Meta is involved. Therefore, different businesses' creations and ideas will work together. Let's have a tour around the various levels and components of this virtual environment, as well as the firms competing with each other and the larger firms' acquisitions and investments.

But, first and foremost, what is the purpose of the metaverse? In the early 90's even science fiction authors could not have foreseen the Instagram Influencers, the United States president tweeting policy or 250 hours of video clips being posted to YouTube per minute. Therefore, we can only make projected estimates! Pokemon Go has over a billion downloads and has been used to walk over 20 billion kilometers only a few years after its inception. In its first month, its wizarding successor made $12 million. Training and education, healthcare, heads-up wayfinding and navigation, tourism, retail, field service, real estate sales, and design and architecture are all examples of where augmented reality is being used. Although these are all one-person experiences, they might evolve into metaverse applications, or a completely new variety of business strategies and experiences could develop.

Data Requirement

The metaverse is deeply rooted in our location. Our experience is shaped by where we are in the universe, not just regarding GPS location but also by our immediate surroundings, whether outside or inside. What room are we in, and who or what things or persons are in our immediate vicinity? What virtual avatars, creatures, information layers, or interactive elements can we find?

As a result, the World Map in the metaverse space is not a 2D or 3D street maps such as Google Maps or Open Street Map. This hyper-local map includes the interiors of rooms, streetscapes, entrances, stairs, surfaces, and their connections — an unbelievable degree of detail! Even though it is insane, firms are already mapping it. Existing mapping like Google Maps, Earth, Street View, Apple Maps and the Indoor Maps Program, and Bing Maps provide incumbents with an advantage, but there are other major geographic data companies like Foursquare and OpenStreetMap.

Supplementing this will be persistent, domain-specific geographic Assets and Data, many static and many immersive with their behaviors. They might be levels of information like guidelines, recommendations, tourist guides, information about things in the environment, game characters, art pieces, or virtual landscapes. They will constitute the content of this digital paradigm: media linked to a physical location, available to be mixed and enjoyed by individuals in the same region, much how webpages today may integrate assets from all over the internet.

Scape, which creates centimeter-level positioning, and ContextGrid, which creates an open registry for AR assets in locations, are two companies looking to hold a piece of the metaverse data. Both Azure Spatial Anchors and Google Cloud Anchors are utilizing their current mapping strengths to drive metaverse adoption.

A Social Graph is also interconnected, including people's identities and connections. Multiplayer game industry giants such as Sony, Activision Blizzard, or EA, or 3D-specific innovations like Aura's "avatar as a service," may be seeking to upset giants such as Meta, Google, Apple, Microsoft, or Snap.

Technology Stack

To join in the metaverse, what devices and technology will we require?

Meta is set to launch its AR Oculus gadget. Beginning with the device itself, in the future, we may be using a headset, glasses, or audio-only wearables with various forms of control or head/gaze tracking. In the meantime, we have Microsoft Hololens, Google Glass, and many other iOS and Android smartphones and tablets.

We anticipate that a real-time Run-Time Platform will power metaverse applications on the gadget. In one scenario, an augmented reality browser similar to today's web browsers, such as WebXR on Chrome, may be used. In a different scenario, game engines such as Unity or Unreal will be dominant. ARKit and ARCore are available for iOS and Android, and there are already established AR platforms such as Wikitude. Microsoft's AltspaceVR and Escher are two examples of recent acquisitions (Niantic).

For metaverse applications, sensing the environment surrounding you will be critical for mapping and localization and identifying objects, environments, and other individuals. This is one of the most important new features required, and it builds on developments in deep learning and computer vision and localization and mapping techniques. It is a strongly competitive business, with a flurry of new startups and acquisitions vying for a piece of one of two emerging sectors with similar sensing requirements.

The several overlapping innovators in this field make it difficult to categorize them. 6D.AI is a well-known firm, and the following are some recent examples:

Simultaneous Localization and Mapping (SLAM)

Here are some leaders in the area of SLAM: Visualix, Kudan, Jido, Augmented Pixels, Blue Vision Labs (bought by Lyft), Dent Reality, Fantasmo, Sturfee, Insider Navigation, Immersal, Scape, Google's Visual Positioning System, 13th Lab (purchased by Meta), Infinity AR (acquired by Alibaba).

Vision Processing

Flyby (purchased by Apple), Regaind, Dreambit (purchased by Meta), RealFace (purchased by Apple), Matrix Mill (purchased by Niantic), Obvious Engineering (bought by Snap), and Cimagine are examples of vision processing technologies required for the metaverse.

There are equally underlying depth mapping technologies like Intel RealSense, Microsoft Kinect, Leap Motion, Occipital, Apple TrueDepth (with related acquisitions such as PrimeSense and LinX), Nimble VR (purchased by Meta), and Apple.

When working at scale, metaverse systems will interact with infrastructure and networks, imposing massive bandwidth, latency, and local processing needs (on devices themselves and the edge of the cloud). The mobile edge computing standards and future fifth-generation networks' potential will be tested here. However, we would hope to see existing edge providers such as Cloudflare, Fastly, and Akamai, as well as major cloud providers like Amazon, Google, and Microsoft, as well as a slew of open-source tools for automation, deployment, caching, federated learning, serverless computing, etc. The concept of hyperlocal maps and meshes will seamlessly integrate into the dispersed edge computing and storage realm.

The metaverse applications, components, and objects outlined above might be supplied worldwide via a distributed network from a few closed central systems. This is a tremendous opportunity for tech-savvy individuals and entrepreneurs to create a niche for themselves in the evolving virtual space.

Tools

Authoring tools, including apps, behaviors, asset creation, and environment development, must be included in the metaverse ecosystem. We will see big platforms such as Unity, Unreal, and Autodesk to maintain their dominance and get creative with projects such as EditorXR or MARS. We can also expect more niche offerings like Torch, Sketchbox, and Dotty AR for sharing models, Cognitive3D for analytics, Anything World for voice interaction, and Blippar's Blippbuilder to arise. RealityKit (Apple), Maquette (Microsoft), Spark AR Studio (Meta), Spatial Workstation for immersive audio (Meta via the acquisition of Two Big Ears), Lens Studio (Snap), and Tiltbrush (Google) are just some of the tools that the big tech companies will use to attract creators. Filming and asset development will be enabled by tools such as Digital Catapult's volumetric capture studio Dimension.

What is the best way for individuals to find your product, content, or application after you have generated it? Like today's app stores or search engines, search tools will have to arise, but we may still be too early for that.

Lastly, what types of metaverse transactions can be expected? The metaverse will allow the sale of apps or content layers, asset or avatar marketplaces, user trade, ownership of physical-world settings, and, definitely, advertising. Arcona, Database, and AR Grid are just a few of the companies looking into this area.

Metaverse Context

The metaverse will unfold within a larger context. Regulation is an obvious factor to consider. How can we keep participants safe if they are playing a game that tempts them to visit actual-world locations? Is it possible that certain publicly accessible areas are indecent or offensive? Is an AR application accountable if it allows users to physically infringe, or just adds virtual content if my ownership of land, property, or landmarks in the physical world translates to the metaverse? Is there a new level of privacy concern if every gadget has biometrics, cameras continuously scanning, or even facial recognition? It may take some time for the world's legal systems to catch up. The "mirrorworld bill of rights," the recent XR Privacy Summit, and this AR Privacy and Security overview from W3C working groups are only the beginning of the public dialogue.

Standards will be developed in tandem to aid development and interoperability. We now have W3C's WebXR, Khronos' OpenXR, Apple and Pixar's USDZ file format, ETSI's 5G MEC, OGC's ARML, and MPEG's ARAF, but it is still early days. There is an issue with the growth of 3D model formats such as gITF, FBX, OBJ, and COLLADA. Interoperability is being promoted by industry associations such as Open AR Cloud.

Finally, there will be patterns and norms. In both the actual and virtual environments, how will we engage? Will we standardize gestures or certain attributes? Will there be commonly used icons or representations? And what will be the social norms? Parallels like recording indications (already incorporated on Snap Spectacles) or audio clicks when shooting images have been suggested by Matt Miesnieks. Will there be something like robots.txt files to restrict how your physical property is scanned, rather than whether search engines can index your website?

Ethics in the Metaverse

A major source of worry in the metaverse is how to prevent toxicity or poor conduct in which people harass or intimidate others. Because many will be in the metaverse, it is obligatory upon its builders to make it a safe area for everybody. For example, people's opinions about sexuality might alter throughout time.

The difficulty had also evolved since, when we initially began with these internet experiences, whether virtualized or not, they did not incorporate as much of the actual world as they do now. The situation has changed. The metaverse will soon be a lot more like being in the actual world. There are issues we have to go through that no one else has gone through.

People will act if they see the metaverse as an add-on to reality rather than reality itself. Non-player characters may become more realistic, or perhaps smarter, in the future. According to Bartle, they may exhibit self-awareness. This might happen in the next few years, and it will take quantum computing to accomplish.

This poses a slew of ethical concerns. Are you going to eliminate the AI folks by erasing the database or turning it off? You might be able to resurrect them or at least duplicate them. Or do you destroy them by duplicating them? Have you become a mass killer if you develop a virtual environment for the sole purpose of killing characters?

You will then select the universe you want to visit, which might be social or gaming realms. We will see a slew of small worlds or metaverses. A translation mechanism might be used to transport objects across metaverse worlds.

You have to respect your players. Because you cannot leave the actual world if you do not like it, you will not be able to travel to another world where you do not have white hair. You have no choice but to remain in this reality. However, reality necessitates competition. You can always "go" to someone else's world if world operators surround you. You will have to respect them, or they will end up playing for someone else.

Simply, players want a place where they can be happy and be their best versions. In the physical world, the dice roll defines you. You do not have to be yourself in the virtual environment. You can uncover who you truly are. That is the kind of thing you would like to be able to see in the future.

Protocol Requirement Solution

With so many possibilities in the metaverse, it is no surprise that so many technological behemoths continue to spend substantially on its growth. Because of the enormous potential influence, many people feel that this will be the next large-scale technology after the internet.

However, creating the "next internet" is easier said than done. Technical support for multiple dimensions and purposes, such as the ideal business economy, payment system, website economy, and other Web 3.0 aspects, is necessary to create the metaverse.

As a Polkadot-based cross-chain protocol, X Protocol intends to fill this need. Polkadot (DOT) is a system that enables multiple blockchains to communicate in a similar way to the traditional internet by connecting different networks using Wanchain's decentralized bridges, a blockchain network interoperability framework. X Protocol thinks that by utilizing these elements, they will realize their goal of creating a "decentralized Metaverse based on Web 3.0."

To enter the metaverse, the X Protocol leverages Web 3.0. The protocol will establish a fair and decentralized standard for all economic activity while ensuring that any firm can freely distribute content. As a result, users may compare the X Protocol public chain to Ethereum (ETH), a blockchain well-known for its smart contract capabilities.

According to X Protocol, the focus has shifted to the basic layer one infrastructure, which comprises source-generated games and lands models. The project is written in RUST and revolves around the Polkadot and Solana (SOL) environment, comprising the protocol and application layers. The layers' major goals are to get organic traffic in the metaverse using self-developed decentralized apps (DApps) and give third-party DApps zero-barrier access to technological solutions.

X Protocol intends to produce DApps to attract organic users, then incorporate each DApp via metaverse scenarios and give third-party DApps easy access to them; this will eventually result in a metaverse environment with a huge number of participants and use cases. On

Polkadot and Solana, X Protocol is rated one of the top metaverse projects in a group experience, linked wallets, and GitHub code volume.

On the X Protocol, a DeFi cross-chain asset pool is being constructed so that tokens generated on many blockchains may be freely exchanged irrespective of which chain they originate from. The X cross-chain bridge may be used to implement this swap capability on the platform. The X Protocol team believes that their approach will "significantly lower the transaction barrier" and "enhance the trading experience for users."

Innovations Towards Building Mobile Gaming

It is difficult to move around the gaming industry without encountering someone who is discussing the metaverse. Suppose you are unfamiliar with the metaverse idea in games; the most basic explanation is that it is a linked world of virtual environments, similar to what Ernest Cline imagined in his cult novel Ready Player One, which has since been vividly brought to life as a Steven Spielberg movie.

Epic Games launched a $1 billion investment for these linked virtual environments, including $200 million from Sony, bringing the metaverse one step closer to life. According to Epic CEO Tim Sweeney, the metaverse will be constructed through open standards to connect various experiences.

The metaverse is still in its early development, but in the meanwhile, we can see some positive signs and what it might look like in the mobile gaming industry. Therefore, let us look at what features of mobile games are expected to change for the metaverse to come to life.

- **Immersion**

It's not yet clear how deep one will go into the metaverse. According to the Oasis in Ready Player One, it's like a haptic whole-body suit with virtual reality spectacles. On the plus side, we see tremendous advancements in virtual reality technology. Oculus moves away from bulky, Computer-reliant headgear with external tracking and toward more affordable standalone gadgets like the Quest 2 with internal tracking.

Yet, the future of virtual reality appears to be firmly anchored in console, PC, or standalone headsets like the Quest. While augmented reality is the dominating reality on smartphones, smartphones and virtual reality have yet to come together. The rumor mill has gone crazy about creating "Apple Glass" augmented reality technology, but who knows?

Full-body tracking will be required in the metaverse as well. Some innovative advances, like the technology designed in collaboration with the Axis XR Interface system for the newly unveiled Virtual Taekwondo Olympic events, transform the whole body into a controller.

- **Content Delivery Infrastructure**

The smartphone world is almost entirely reliant on Apple and Google for content distribution. Individuals must first download an application, after which they can choose from a variety of payment options. Game streaming, on the other hand, is rapidly evolving. While Google Stadia has had a shaky start in the market, Microsoft has announced Xbox Cloud Gaming, available on mobile devices. This brings us one step closer to the metaverse's promise of smooth mobile streaming experiences. Nevertheless, this necessitates a large amount of high-speed data outside of the home, which would necessitate the widespread deployment of high-speed fifth-generation networks (and beyond), which is still a way off.

- **Open Standards**

If the actual metaverse is to succeed on the internet, it will need to be developed on open standards that link these virtual worlds. This implies that the metaverse is not "owned" by a single entity, which could be troublesome. This open standard is in direct opposition to Apple and Google's present business models, including walled gardens in which they maintain strict control over payments and what can be published. The dispute between Epic and Apple over Fortnite, which ended in the game being removed from the App Store, is the best example of this. Sweeney's larger objectives for the metaverse and Epic's role make his willingness to challenge Apple's dominance a possible barrier to a real metaverse. Finally, the app stores are so profitable for Apple and Google that it would be surprising if they did not adjust to changing market models if their dominance changed.

Recently, mobile games, particularly Chinese applications with specific hangout social spaces, have seen a surge in social functionalities. Mechanics and co-op gameplay are making their way into even simple games. There has been a rising trend in co-op-style tasks over the past three or more years in the top 100 selling iOS mobile apps.

Roblox and Fortnite, with different in-game offers and promotions, have been the most successful actors in attempting to achieve a full metaverse. Fortnite included a Party Royale feature and a social site called Island in early 2020, albeit it is no more accessible on mobile devices. Fortnite has also shown a season of complete Christopher Nolan films and offered previews of movie trailers like Tenet. Before Party Royale, Fortnite held the huge Travis Scott Astronomical event, drawing 12.3 million viewers.

Roblox has been ambitious in its aim to design the metaverse framework, with co-promotions ranging from Ready Player Two (abandoning their actual goals!), Lil Nas X concert and a Gucci Garden event resulted in virtual products traded for thousands of dollars online. Roblox is the perfect example of how a future smartphone metaverse would appear as it is still a walled garden that would only be a small part of the overall interlinked experience.

- **A Functioning Economy**

This relates to the preceding argument about the walled garden, notably Apple and Google's desire to control the environment and payment mechanism. Roblox rewards developers with Robux and allows individuals to exchange products, yet it maintains a walled garden. A decentralized economy would be required for a genuine metaverse to develop. However, we must tread carefully here, given the gaming industry's reaction to blockchain's environmental consequences and NFTs' huge over-inflation and subsequent collapse. Considering the absence of green credentials and the instability of NFTs, blockchain and decentralized finance offer a blueprint for technology initiatives that could help the metaverse's global economy.

1

MEGATRENDS SHAPING
THE METAVERSE

This chapter outlines some megatrends – global exponential movements now happening — and how they will define the metaverse's future. The majority of the megatrends involve a mix of technological and societal development. We will describe the megatrends as follows.

- **Virtual Mainstreaming**

People are increasingly considering the virtual world to be just as genuine as the physical one. In the real world, trust is essential to the functioning of relationships and systems. It is the foundation for how companies thrive in legal systems, how our money market continues to function, and how we assess our relationships. Each of these technologies is scalable because of trust.

The scalability of the metaverse and the sectors that support it will improve as confidence in the "virtual" domain grows — with online friends, virtual objects and cryptocurrency assets, smart contracts, and live online experiences.

According to Gartner, more than half of big companies will utilize low-code and no-code app platforms (LCAPs) to manage at least part of their systems by 2023. Low-code/no-code app platforms are visual software development systems that let business and individual developers drag and drop app components, link them, and build mobile or web apps. The automation of process, deployment, security, scaling, and interaction with numerous data endpoints accounts for a big part of the "magic" of LCAP. The majority of the time spent creating internet apps is spent dealing with complexity and scale. The outcome will be a substantial decrease in the amount of effort necessary to construct apps, as well as a shift in who conducts the job. Most of the creators are migrating to a serverless system. On the other hand, an expanding number of developer tools make it simple to produce metaverse content, script advanced behaviors, and engage in commerce.

- **Low-Code Platforms**

Low-code and no-code app platforms (LCAP) replace workflows, logic, and apps' hand-coding with greater-level abstractions (like visual scaffolding and drag-and-drop tools). The most evident advantage of this development is that non-programmers can now perform some tasks traditionally performed by programmers. This, nevertheless, does not completely represent the effect or why businesses are using these platforms.

It is common knowledge that goods appeal to either large or small businesses, but this is not always the case. Although it is typically difficult for "business" technology to scale down to individuals, there are several occasions when things have been able to be in the hands of people, which has shown to be the most cost-effective choice for the organization. Recently, no-code/low-code systems such as Shopify have been used to power anything from tiny enterprises to some of the world's top brands (Hasbro, Budweiser, etc.). The metaverse will gradually be constructed by a larger number of producers, with a larger library of plug-in apps and logic to support them.

- **Machine Intelligence**

Computers are taking over more jobs that were previously performed by humans. Deep learning, machine learning, and artificial intelligence are examples of such fields.

We live in a universe where learning programs fine-tune advertising messaging, marketing, and online engagement. Natural language processing and picture recognition are still in their infancy. In the real world, we are getting increasingly close to applications like self-driving cars.

Machine intelligence aligns with all other trends you find in the metaverse. It will influence creativity as machines become players in the creation process — simply look at how AI Dungeon develops tales or how Promethean AI can create a virtual environment — and consider how far this will progress in the next decade.

AI will be utilized to create the metaverse's microchips and produce code to help programmers. Gestures will be interpreted. The movement of our eyes will be predicted, emotions will be recognized, and machines will even recognize the firing of neurotransmitters in our brains.

Machine intelligence will be integrated into our no-code and low-code application systems, where it will serve as a design adviser and a component of the infrastructure. Agents based on our choices and interests will uncover the information we desire whenever we want it. And the places we explore will become more populated by virtual creatures.

- **Cybernetics' Ascension**

The age of cybernetics has come. They are not as well spread as they will be in the future, nor are they as refined and fantastic. The incorporation of human sensory and motor networks with machines is known as cybernetics. Existing examples are used by video game input/output devices, wearables, smartphone accelerometers, and virtual reality headsets.

Because of miniaturization and high-speed networking, devices have evolved from fixed workstations to portable, powerful computers in our pockets. These computers are getting closer to our bodies. We are transitioning from gazing at machines from the outside to inhabiting the virtual world and living in an environment where computing is all around us.

Since these are not phones but powerful supercomputers with a telephony program preloaded, the word "smartphone" already feels outdated. Virtual reality headgear like the Oculus, which reacts to the eyes, head position, and movements, allows us to enter the virtual world already. We will bring this experience to more of the environment around us once these become smartglasses. We could even have working smart contact lenses in the nearest future.

Light field technology might even enable us to transmit photons to the retina, along with their associated depth of field, enabling the eye to concentrate on different portions of a virtual environment, culminating in a fully holographic experience.

Our audio signals, gestures, and biometrics will all be widely interpreted by these gadgets. Neural interfaces may potentially allow gadgets to grasp our intents more quickly than we do. The consequence? The metaverse will be more than just a location we visit. The metaverse will FEEL like us.

And the merging of wearable and mobile technologies represents a societal shift as much as a technological one. It will alter the layout of our houses, public transportation, communities, and employment. It will alter the way you meet people, order food, travel, and cooperate on projects.

- **Open Systems' Challenges**

The Internet was designed to be a decentralized, massively dispersed network of compatible computers and programs. Several extremely big platforms that function as gatekeepers and tollbooths now control the Internet. However, new technologies and open standards are evolving that have the potential to revolutionize the metaverse's future.

WebAssembly (Wasm) claims to create sandboxed binary programs for the open web that are fast and secure. WebGL and WebXR will aid in the creation of graphical and interactive experiences which can be distributed outside of app stores. Platforms such as Unity Data-Oriented Technology Stack (DOTS) leverage these technologies to provide small, fast binaries that operate to the metaverse's expectations (particularly, Project Tiny at Unity).

Since they enable extensive cooperation amongst software engineering projects, open systems are also a social phenomenon. Reed's Law, which forecasted the explosive growth of apps like Slack and WhatsApp, could be applied to the Open-Source revolution, effectively a permissionless social network for software engineers.

Wasm, an open-source and open platform, might increase the number of possible partners, generating more benefit than all of the permissioned platforms put together. Permissionless systems such as Linux and the PC should also survive in the future. Similarly, technology like zero-knowledge proofs and decentralized digital identification systems can let people reclaim control over their data. Since they do not have to trust anyone, customers may be more willing to trust internet apps with their personal information.

If we can free apps and data to achieve this, we have the possibility for a massive increase in network effects.

- **Adoption of the Blockchain**

Blockchain network, a distributed ledger system, can do for assets and data whatever Open Source and the Internet can do for software and apps. Decentralized authority, a record of history and authenticity, and a demonstrable rarity of assets are all possible with a blockchain network. A blockchain enables permissionless involvement or control via a decentralized autonomous organization when it is decentralized.

Blockchains are used for a variety of purposes, one of which is programmability. While programmability is not intrinsic in every blockchain network, it is a significant feature of Ethereum and other "smart contract" chains.

What is the significance of this? It is the network effects at work once more—the greater the value of the network, the greater the nodes that can engage. Similarly, the greater the groups that can develop around various activities (games, financial legos, etc.), the greater the value of the network under Reed's Law. The impact on value is enormous. More people, more apps, and more components to put together mean more smart contracts and decentralized apps.

Since you do not have to trust anyone's authority, blockchain networks are called "trustless" since the trust is placed in the blockchain network itself. The global scalability of blockchain networks is due to the long tail dispersion of all the trustless apps, contracts, and elements.

Decentralized borrowing, decentralized banking, and decentralized asset exchanges have benefited from network effects, which have opened the way for on-chain data feeds (oracles) that may be utilized as conditions in smart contracts. The growth of NFTs may form the fundamental of virtual commodities in a new generation of games, avatar modifications, and metaverse space, as blockchain computing eliminates some components of cloud computing.

The possibilities are endless when assets, data, and programmable contracts are released onto the open internet.

- **Walled Garden Ecosystem**

Every other megatrend that affects the metaverse favors Walled Gardens — and we use this phrase with affection since gardens may be attractive and well-organized. Not all applications or worlds will be accessible. Permission, integration, curation, and control are all qualities that might be useful in a platform or application. Without the combination of these qualities, Roblox would never have been as popular.

Interestingly, the open systems that threaten them are also beneficial to walled gardens. Most users may feel safer since they use the same open-source and blockchain network as everyone else. It is not difficult to have a walled garden. The problem with the existing environment of 2021 is that there are too few walled gardens. It should be simple to design your walled garden and allow other developers to join in, add to, change, and integrate with your rules.

As the number of walled gardens grows, the question of how each will be identified arises. Roblox, for example, is a hierarchy discovery system that functions as a "YouTube for games," powered by search and appeal. This will continue because individuals enjoy curating and creators enjoy having access to vast audiences. However, technologies for portable avatars, portable social networks, and interoperability are under development. This might help connect diverse walled gardens utilizing open platforms while also allowing discovery and curation options.

We might have a hypermedia-like architecture in the nearest future, with portals connecting many environments and experiences — the virtual environment's analog of hyperlinks on websites.

- **Distributed Networks Acceleration**

By orders of magnitude, fifth-generation networks will increase mobile networking performance, concurrency, and latency. Within a decade, we should witness 10 Gbps speeds with 1ms latency. And the fifth-generation network is not the end of the road: the sixth-generation network will boost these figures by 10–100X.

Increasing speeds are required to sustain the metaverse. Still, the network effects occur when all network users can exchange real-time data that provide some of the most intriguing possibilities.

Because the local network layer is no more the barrier, the attention will turn to deliver additional processing power to the network's "far" edge. This may occur at a nearby cell tower, or it may occur directly inside your house, where data will be preprocessed and displayed on your cybernetic gadgets.

Because it will be too slow to interpret information in a remote/centralized way, most artificial intelligence that drives apps will happen on edge. The constellation of local computer devices and data sources must interoperate fast in the future. For uses in the metaverse wherein predictions of behaviors and physics are good enough, this will occasionally mean prediction at the edge.

- **Replicating Reality**

For years, a combination of hacks known as shader programming was used to produce real-time visuals in practically every game using 3D graphics. Ray tracing simulates how pictures appear based on how photons bounce across and through different materials using the physics of light. Ray tracing can produce significantly more attractive and realistic graphics, employing pre-rendered content like movies. Still, it necessitates a significant increase in computing power. Real-time raytracing, on the other hand, is on the way.

It is only one of the ways we will be replicating reality in our machines. For instance, one of NVIDIA's Omniverse platform's applications is modeled fluid dynamics: consider being able to realistically portray a river or an HVAC system (which may be used to know how strong a structure is in a pandemic involving a respiratory disease). Consider all these models and artificial intelligence engines connected to a common framework that enables logic and prediction to replicate a universe of virtual computers, objects, places, and people.

Data will equally be collected from an ever-increasing number of real-world channels. Geospatial and traffic data; digital twins of real items that are initialized to report all of their features; oracles that provide financial data to smart contracts; and real-world data on individuals and processes are examples.

We will not just have an Internet of Things; we will have an Internet of Everything, with predictive analytics, artificial intelligence, and real-world visualization. These breakthroughs will allow a metaverse to layer over and simulate the physical world and power the next generation of physics-based games that are more stunning and engaging than anything seen before.

The metaverse will change how we interact, work, and play; the megatrends we have mentioned can help you see how.

2

MAIN METAVERSE PROJECTS

Top Metaverse Projects to Invest in

Since you have every reason to think that the metaverse is becoming a reality, now is the best moment to invest in blockchain-based metaverse projects. However, do you know which blockchain-based metaverses are the best? Do you know how to get yourself into one? If you don't, then you should read this section carefully. We have discussed the top 5 metaverse projects to invest in:

- **Enjin (MetaCity)**

MetaCity is the world's first free-to-earn NFT real estate, influenced by the game Minecraft. Metacity currently has only 70 NFT plots accessible for owners to create a variety of firms.

Metacity is one of the popular games because of the free NFT drops that you may earn, market, or keep forever. It also allows users to play different games at the same time. This implies that customers will be able to swap stuff across the two games, MetaCity and Minecraft, in this case.

Another intriguing feature of the game is its creator economy. By simply doing what you enjoy, you add value to the world and make a living. In the MetaCity, for instance, anybody will be able to: Create nonfungible token characters and nonfungible token art exhibitions.

Have you heard of the wildly popular Grand Theft Auto server game? Did you know it is now possible to play it within the Enjin Metaverse? MetaCity's Fractured Lands NFT properties became live recently. The benefit of this platform is that it allows users to spend their cryptocurrency assets within MetaCity. This implies that participants can claim a piece of land, and a nonfungible token will be created to show its worth.

Finally, anybody may begin playing the game for free and collect capital coins to purchase NFT plots on the Minecraft server. Currently, just that server is available. It is vital to note that purchasing NFT plots is currently unavailable. This function will be available shortly.

- **Sandbox**

The Sandbox is a virtual environment built on the Ethereum blockchain network where gamers create, control, and monetize their gaming time. The idea is to upset established game producers such as Minecraft and Roblox by giving creators true ownership in the form of non-fungible tokens and compensating them for their contributions to the environment.

The Sandbox is one of the top five Metaverse projects, according to CoinGecko, accounting for 7% of the market. The Sandbox's framework for creating games within the metaverse is one of the reasons you will like it. Users that create content using blockchain networks and smart contracts will have a better experience with it. The Sandbox Game Maker exemplifies it.

The Sandbox also contains a tool called VoxEdit that allows anybody to begin producing objects. Imagine how much fun it would be to make 3D assets. VoxEdit allows users to post, publish, and sell NFT creations.

When completed, assets can be sold by posting an initial selling offer on the NFT marketplace, where interested purchasers can bid on them. In addition, The Sandbox will shortly launch a limited-time experience called "Main Hub." This will be a gathering spot where people may mingle. We are sure you have seen the series "The Walking Dead." On the other hand, this franchise has purchased a property in Sandbox to provide a fantastic experience for its customers. If you wish to buy land in the "Walking Dead" zone, follow this guide.

Snoop Dog is in The Sandbox, which is one piece of evidence that this metaverse is growing in mainstream popularity. He will have a residence and an exclusive NFT collection to conduct live concerts and interact with gamers.

The Sandbox's governance token, $SAND, serves as the transaction's backbone. This enables participants to, among other things, access the site, play games, stake money, and receive prizes. More than 20 exchanges have listed the $SAND token. Crypto.com, Polionex, Bittrex, and Kraken are just a few of the most well-known exchanges.

How to Participate in the Sandbox

By the end of the year, the Sandbox will be released. Nevertheless, you may now purchase a parcel on OpenSea in the meantime. The pre-season 0 activities will be available first to landowners. Other players will be able to pre-register and gain entry to the event as time goes on. You are welcome to add your name to the whitelist.

To get started, go to The Sandbox's official website and look at the Map section. On the first day of the activities, much of the map will be obscured by fog. The fog will be lifted, and experiences will be unlocked systematically throughout several weeks of the event. The Sandbox Marketplace also has a large selection of nonfungible tokens to choose from.

- **Ultra**

Ultra is the pioneer fee-free blockchain network ecosystem of its type, enabling an entertainment platform that brings together diverse gaming sectors and blockchain-driven services in one place. Ultra's network will be able to handle more than 12,000 transactions per second.

Ultra will offer you access to a wide range of centralized and decentralized services, including the ability to find, purchase, play, and sell games and in-game stuff, watch live-streaming feeds, communicate with your desired influencers, enter contests, participate in tournaments, and many more.

Ultra, however, has its own ERC-20 coin, $UOS. Uniswap, Bitfinex, Bitrue, Kucoin, and Bancor Network are all places where you can buy $UOS. Transactions on Ultra are also free and very instantaneous. Anybody can stake $UOS and get exceedingly limited edition NFTs as a reward. When the system becomes congested, users' transactions are placed in a queue that automatically prioritizes them. The users who have invested the most $UOS tokens will be moved to the head of the line.

How to Participate in Ultra

Ultra is still in beta. The official release, however, will happen shortly. The beta version contains three stages that must be completed in that sequence. The first phase started in December 2020. The Ultra Platform is a downloadable program that includes an Ultra wallet and access to the Ultra blockchain-powered application ecosystem. Participants will be able to download the wallet-only software after the Mainnet has been connected to the Ultra platform.

All of the participant's favorite programs may be found in one spot. They interact with entertainment services utilizing future DeFi apps in a variety of ways, from playing games to trading on nonfungible token marketplaces. To open an account today, you must first download the wallet.

- **Chiliz**

Chiliz is now a member of the Sandbox Metaverse. Chiliz has

reportedly bought 576 acres in The Sandbox. In The Sandbox metaverse, Chiliz will create a sports and entertainment community for supporters of partner teams like FC Barcelona, Juventus, and Paris Saint-Germain. Via Fan Tokens, Chiliz enables athletic organizations to communicate with and profit from their global fan base.

There is currently no fixed date for Chiliz's lands on Sandbox to open. You must first establish a Sandbox account, then look for and engage with Chiliz lands.

- **Sorare**

Sorare is a blockchain-based nonfungible token football game. On the Sorare platform, more than 180 football teams are fully licensed, with additional clubs entering each week. Sorare is a fantastic investment option because it allows users to build a fantasy squad using their purchased cards. Each card is a representation of a real person. Cardholders will get points depending on the success of that player on the real pitches. As a prize, the teams with the most points each week will make new cards.

Sorare, however, has declared a Serie B investment of $680 million. Furthermore, did you realize that the "Lionel Messi" nonfungible token cost 7.9 ETH to buy? Ubisoft has produced a game using Sorare's nonfungible tokens, which is another Sorare-related narrative.

Finally, you may open a free account with your email address and begin partaking in Sorare. Sorare nonfungible token cards may be purchased via bank transfer or debit/credit cards. Apple Pay and Android Pay are also available. Sorare nonfungible token cards are available for purchase in more than 40 countries.

Top Metaverse Token to Invest in

Although there are many methods to invest in the metaverse and get a cut of the pie, we will focus on blockchain-based digital tokens in this article. Blockchain network technology will certainly power metaverse systems, allowing users to own, develop, and exchange digital assets utilizing NFTs and cryptocurrencies such as bitcoin and ether.

Nonfungible tokens have aided the metaverse's recent surge in popularity. So, what are some of the most important metaverse tokens to be aware of?

- **Meta Tokenized Stock**

Meta Tokenized Stocks are transferable tokens representing the underlying asset's value, which works similarly to stablecoins. It is the creation and issuance of digital tokens or "coins" that reflect an individuals' equity shares in a business or organization. In contrast, a stock (sometimes called equity) is only a financial instrument that reflects ownership of a part of a company.

Mark Zuckerberg wants Meta to transform into a metaverse firm. As a result, it is no surprise that Meta has made significant investments in the metaverse. The internet behemoth has so far put $50 million into its 'XR Programs and Research Fund' metaverse initiatives.

Put another way. Meta Tokenized Stock (FB) are tokenized derivatives that reflect traditional securities. They are a tokenized copy of stock that is usually backed 1:1 by the underlying stock. With all of Meta's funds going into the metaverse, buying Meta Tokenized Stock might be quite profitable in a few years.

Using the Meta tokenized stock, you may decide to purchase a fraction of an item rather than the whole stock. It has better liquidity than other real stocks based on where you live, and they may be exchanged all round the clock against real Meta stock.

You may buy Meta tokenized stocks on FTX and Bittrex.

- **Decentralized (MANA)**

MANA, Decentraland's token, is another metaverse token you ought to be aware of. Decentraland is a VR platform built on the blockchain network that allows participants to purchase, trade, and develop land while playing games, generating content, and communicating with other participants.

The largest virtual world in the nonfungible token realm is Decentraland, which is denoted by the non-fungible ERC-71 token LAND. On Decentraland, each piece of land is unique, and its owners have complete control over what they do with it.

MANA is a platform that allows a participant to buy land. MANA is the primary token in Decentraland, and it is used to acquire land as well. It is used to pay for products and services since it is a native utility token. It is likewise based on Ethereum, and it may be purchased and traded in exchange for other crypto or fiat money. The overall supply of MANA has been set at 2.6 billion. This implies that at any point in time, there will never be more than 2.6 billion MANA.

- **Axie Infinite (AXS)**

The Ethereum-supported digital currencies AXS and SLP are used in Axie Infinity, an online video game based on NFTs. In this play-to-earn game, players breed, grow, and combat their digital pets, called Axies. AXS is the native token in the Axie Infinity game.

Holders of tokens can vote and influence the game's course. Unlike typical games, where the game creators make all the decisions, this is a collaborative effort. AXS token holders can vote on various governance initiatives in addition to staking their tokens and earning more.

Smooth Love Potion (SLP) token is also used in the Axie world. The primary use of the SLP token is for breeding reasons. Winning adventures and fights in the game will gain the SLP token. The SLP token is distinct from the AXS token in that it is not a native token. As a result, it is not utilized in votes. A total of 270 million AXS tokens are available.

- **Enjin Coin (ENJ)**

You might also check out Enjin Coin, which is a metaverse token. It is an Ethereum-based token designed to use nonfungible tokens as simple as possible for people, brands, and enterprises. Nonfungible tokens developed using Enjin, on the other hand, employ the ERC-1155 standard, which is not the same as the ERC-721 standard.

ENJ is the governance token on the platform. ENJ directly backs nonfungible tokens that are created in the Enjin ecosystem. A fixed quantity of ENJ is created into each new nonfungible token created on the network. The locked funds determine the freshly created tokens' physical-world value. Enjin also received about $19 million lately, which will be utilized to develop a Polkadot-based blockchain for nonfungible tokens. A total of one billion ENJ tokens are available.

- **The Sandbox (SAND)**

The Sandbox is a virtual environment based on the Ethereum blockchain network, just like the other platforms in this book. Participants may create, monetize, and control their own game experiences on the platform. The SAND token, an ERC-20 utility token for governance, staking, and transfers, is utilized on the network. SAND is another token to keep an eye on in the metaverse, with a maximum supply of 3 billion tokens.

- **Atlas Stars (ATLAS)**

In a virtual gaming metaverse, Star Atlas is a massive online multiplayer game. The game uses Unreal Engine 5 to create real-time, cinematic settings. Three big groups compete for dominance and resources in the game. The game also includes role-playing and is partially a flying simulator.

Players will utilize the ATLAS tokens in the Star Atlas game, presently being developed on the Solana blockchain. The in-game money will be ATLAS tokens, which can be used to acquire assets and nonfungible tokens on the NFT marketplace. A total of 36 billion ATLAS tokens are available for purchase.

- **Metaverse Index (MVI)**

Another fascinating example of a metaverse token is the Metaverse Index (MVI). The coin is created to capture the shift in commerce, entertainment, and sport moving to virtual environments and is represented by an ERC20 token.

Owners of the MVI token have access to a wide range of tokens from several cryptocurrency projects, including online games, non-fungible tokens, and virtual environments. Consider the Metaverse Index token to be a metaverse ETF for cryptocurrency. There are a total of 39,602 Metaverse Index tokens in circulation.

Metaverse Token Rise

The race for the metaverse is starting to heat up now that Facebook has formally rebranded as "Meta." However, metaverse pioneers do not appear to be in danger based on token pricing.

The Metaversal Index, which includes 14 assets linked to the hype-laden paradigm, is up 13.7 percent immediately after the public announcement. As of Oct. 28, 2021, the index's greatest winner was MANA, which had gained 48.9%.

The Metaversal Index's double-digit 24-hour rise outperforms Ethereum's 9.6% gain. As of Oct. 28, 2021, the cryptocurrency market was up 6.2 percent overall. Investors appear to be viewing Facebook's rebranding and accompanying hour-and-seventeen-minute presentation as a positive sign rather than a death knell for Web3's metaversal goals.

"Meta is quite positive about cryptocurrency. There is no world where web3 does not drive the metaverse. Cooper Turley, a partner at cryptocurrency fund Variant Fund and a Defiant contributor, stated, "Today, the world's largest social network just confirmed that future." Some people are reacting negatively to Meta's rebranding. "The stakes are bigger than ever; the aims are clearer," said Jeffrey Zirlin, co-founder of Axie Infinity, whose AXS token holds the Metaversal

Index's biggest allocation at 24.5 percent as of Oct. 28. "This is a fight for liberty." Do not let them take control of our movement."

It is still unclear how Meta plans to handle the metaverse. Interestingly, Meta CEO Mark Zuckerberg stated that building the diverse experiences of a virtual environment will involve hundreds of thousands of producers and creators working together. Even more crypto-forward principles such as interoperability, or the ability to move your digital products from one application to another, were underlined by Zuckerberg.

Meta also makes the Oculus Rift headset. Web3 has not developed anything nearly competitive in hardware, which is a need of the metaverse. The old corporations and organizations that cryptocurrency is attempting to replace have an odd relationship with it. On the one hand, the legendary Christie's art house is known for its NFT auctions. On the other hand, Christie's is a gatekeeper to the art world, normally exclusively available to the rich elite.

With Meta, a similar scenario might be at play. They are confirming the metaverse concept, but the devil is in the details of how they interface with web3 NFTs and protocols. Zuckerberg is using some of the crypto lingoes.

In any case, Meta shareholders were just as pleased as web3 token holders, with the company's price up 1.47 percent.

3

BUSINESS MODELS
IN THE METAVERSE

Many businesses have come and gone in virtual environments. Some have made investments in their own virtual environments, while others have made investments in their presence in virtual environments. In this section, we would want to go through some of the ways people and organizations have experimented with the metaverse, compiling a list of successful business models.

- **Inworld Economy**

This is the manufacture and sale of virtual goods and services for actual money to Avatars. In-world companies have been enormously profitable, with a few people making five to six figures from these virtual goods. Only in the metaverse can you find these things and services. Anshe Chung's 'Dreamland' - Virtual Real Estate, Strokerz Toys - Sex toys and body parts, and Solange - Designing virtual, digital fashion are examples of these enterprises.

- **Business Integration**

When dealing with one-to-one or one-to-many communications, virtual environments offer their own set of benefits. E-mail, Skype, and Instant Messengers have all become part of our daily work routine. Some businesses are testing the market to see what virtual environments can accomplish for them—using communication's capabilities to expedite management, internal education, business-to-business communication, or any other use cases to assist an organization's business operations. IBM, for instance, is developing its own 'metaverse,' while Cisco uses the virtual world for internal communication.

- **Inworld Economy Brand Presence/Avartising**

Build an offline brand in the metaverse and promote real-world items to avatars and virtual individuals. This model has received the most media attention and has already experienced a lot of "trial and error." Because of the unsuccessful trials with merely brand presence, metaverse skeptics claim that virtual environments (metaverse) are not viable commercial platforms. There are many examples, but lingerie company Carnal and the television show 'The L-Word' are two of the most fascinating.

- **Content Development**

Businesses, on the whole, lack the knowledge to develop a 3D presence. They provide guidance and assist in creating virtual experiences through which other businesses may express their brand presence. Millions of Us, for example, has developed islands for Pontiac, HBO, and Intel. Other firms have specialized in 3D communications and content creation for these businesses.

- **Virtual Entrepreneurial Services**

The buzz around virtual environments is not simply attracting those who want to generate content for them. New use cases and offerings have been developed to help all of these internet businesses. The Electric Sheep company's theLoop lists popular destinations on a website, and numerous mashups merge the metaverse client with web 2.0 apps like Twitter and WordPress.

- **Create Your Virtual Environment**

Another option we would want to discuss is the numerous 'brand worlds' that firms have developed. Users may connect and play in a branded world to build brand loyalty in their niches. They uniquely interact with the brand, resulting in 'preferred advertising,' or advertisements they specifically watch. Barbie World and Coca-Cola's Coke Studios' are two examples.

Metanomics

To begin, Doug Thompson coined the term 'metanomics' regarding virtual environments and their economies over a decade ago. He hosted a show in Second Life and a set of podcasts on the subject.

A nightclub in the video game Entropia Universe was auctioned for $635,000 in 2010. In Second Life, the digital version of Amsterdam was auctioned for $50,000 in 2007. In the same year, an elf named Zeuzo was acquired for $9,500 in World of Warcraft. For managing somebody's identity over an hour, a 21-year-old received $125, and a 16-year-old earned $3 million in the Fortnite World Cup.

Do you need more examples?

In 2009, a group of creative gamers in EVE Online invented the E-Bank. They essentially built a Vostro account structure, which is analogous to physical world central banks. They provided loans, paid interest, had a CEO, a board of directors, and everything was really well organized. The CEO then stole 200 billion ISK (the EVE currency) and exchanged it for almost 6,000 Australian dollars.

This is metanomics - the metaverse's economy — and it is happening right now all around us.

2.5 billion individuals interact in virtual worlds using their smartphones, consoles, laptops, desktops, and virtual reality headsets while living and exchanging money online. We are watching something that will have a real-world impact on society and economics, collapsing the barriers between the two spheres. What occurs in one will impact the other; millionaires will be created, and businesses will bankrupt. The epidemic has served as a true litmus test for how closely the two worlds are intertwined – metanomics is an asymmetric hedge against actual-world occurrences. When things are going well, the virtual economy thrives, but when things aren't, it may shine as a source of amusement and community, fully self-contained and unaffected by the outside world.

The creator economy, NFTs, and distributed ledger-based marketplaces that let users purchase, sell, and trade are all the rage right now. The nonfungible token market volume is reportedly over $700 million, and OpenSea is on its way to a $100 billion value in record time. Ethereum blockchain-based markets look to be gaining traction as a critical foundation for metaverse economics, but something is missing at the moment.

Scarcity

People flock to virtual game products markets for a variety of reasons. There is a scarcity of usefulness, as well as a scarcity of interconnected economies. According to Vili Lehdonvirta of the Oxford Internet Institute's digital economies team, uUsers purchase virtual commodities for the same reasons they purchase real items: status, recognition, and belonging to certain subgroups and communities.

Digital products are purchased and traded; it is a speculative market, but you do not have much control over what you possess. You must be able to do something with your asset ownership to generate functional economies in the metaverse. If you buy a new dining table from a market, you want to use it to equip a digital house. All you can do right now is appreciate your buy on OpenSea or another website and tell everyone the URL. Presently, there is nothing to do. The absence of open utility right now (this does not include purchasing things within another metaverse's walled garden as that is what they are designed for) will be a problem for a long time, particularly as the sector grapples with standards and interoperability issues. Tim Sweeney estimates that we will be in for at least 5–10 years of agony on that front, and if he is right, the delay will effectively extinguish virtual economies.

Furthermore, the promise of distributed ledger-based exchanges and the development of multiple cryptocurrencies that power them should make it simple to transfer the value of products and services across various metaverses. However, we are still a long way from realizing this ideal.

It is reminiscent of when companies used initial coin offerings (ICOs) to raise funds for their businesses. Different virtual environments are being created, each with its token-based economy, but there is no true linked exchange of value or assets between them. For instance, if you wanted to exchange your plot of land in Decentraland for a piece of land in Ember Swords, it may be utterly useless. Similarly, the processes for purchasing, selling, and trading on exchanges necessitate a basic grasp of cryptocurrencies and the use of software such as Metamask. Altcoins must first be changed into Ethereum or another well-known crypto, then back into an altcoin from another metaverse to trade, paying a charge each time. We are in the early stages of developing a working exchange market that is as easy to use as fiat money but excludes many individuals who would like to partake in the metaverse but do not know how metanomics works.

This is particularly the case when individuals open eBay businesses to sell digital products and unique objects, which is another place where the two worlds converge. There is no use in having virtual goods if you cannot exchange them openly in the physical world.

Demand and Supply

We mean that for economies to work, we must consider consumption, destruction, and material rarity. The principle underlining it is that, if you buy a virtual product with your digital currency — say, a scarce virtual schoolhouse that stays on your game board within a game, and you pay $5 for it — the simple truth is that, as a user, even if the terms of service describe that the social-gaming corporation has no obligation to the user after that transaction takes place, as a user, when you log in the next day, into the game, you expect the schoolhouse to be there. It will continue to be on your game board as long as you keep playing the game. By the same token, if you buy virtual gas for your virtual car, the money is not collected until you utilize the virtual gas for your vehicle until it is consumed. So, the core principle is that income is recognized when virtual products are sold rather than when virtual money is sold. However, revenue recognition begins when the virtual currency is turned into a virtual product. You recognize durable things ratably throughout their projected useful lives and consumable items, like virtual gas, as they are spent.

This follows the MMO video game economics, yet it plays a significant role in the metaverse environment. Individuals will be pushed to create with the resources available in the metaverse they want to live in, much like a working economy in the real world.

EVE Online is perhaps the greatest example of a working economy in a virtual setting. It easily outperforms Second Life. It is initially and foremost a video game, but it is also a metaverse.

Dr. Gumundsson and his team of economists administer and lead the EVE Online economy. They created the market so that there is an infinite quantity of material to gather across the virtual world in which it is located. Collecting materials, on the other hand, costs time and money. In other words, there are always trade-offs and opportunity costs while acquiring materials. Materials acquired gain value as a result of these trade-offs.

Eve Online's in-game economy is a free market that players mostly drive. NPC merchants offer skill books, which players utilize to gain new talents and blueprints for building ships and modules. Players may mine resources, make new commodities, exchange virtual assets for services, and form contracts. In EVE, there is a well-functioning political structure between groups of players and the factions to which they belong.

NPC merchants also purchase and sell trade products – this truly distinguishes the game and a notion for metanomics — that AI-driven players are always driving the economy ahead.

In EVE, it seems like both game theory and auction theory may be tested. EVE appears to be based on physical-world microeconomic principles, according to the data. Additionally, the data reveal a supply-and-demand connection that is consistent with microeconomic theory.

Eve Online Economics

EVE Online may be an exception, but economists have studied it for years to determine why it works so effectively. While some of the ideas discussed previously, such as material deterioration and scarcity, do not exist in EVE, they are traits that, if brought to a metaverse, may very well drive the metanomics of the virtual environment in which it is situated.

You may give EVE gamers a shovel and expect them to dig a hole, but instead, they will disassemble it and turn it into a hammock.

Star Wars Galaxies is another remarkable example of a player-powered open economy that enables the development of assets to the point where many are unique – similar to what we are witnessing now with the nonfungible token market. A distributed system might allow the development and registration of new products that consume resources inside the metaverse. The blueprint could serve as a license and a way for the developer to earn money by selling it to others. As a result, a reseller market or a manufacturing method would emerge, consuming resources and employing people to produce and sell the commodities.

If the metaverse seems much like the physical environment, some of the virtual environments we will see emerge will become just as useful. Individuals will live and work there instead of outside.

Within the metaverse, metanomics presents a significant opportunity. We are still learning how to manage rich and robust economies within these virtual environments and how one might possibly impact the other and the rest of the world.

However, if it takes a group of economists to operate the economy in only one game, imagine the difficulty that each metaverse entrepreneur would have in attempting to establish a working economy in their own reality — and we have to think about this beyond just setting up a cryptocurrency-exchange for nonfungible tokens.

Using the Metaverse to Benefit Your Business

To benefit from the metaverse, you must ensure that your design is completely optimized for human motivation. The days of firms relying only on the value proposition of their products to gain customers and convince them to purchase goods and services are long gone.

Your product or service's design should be so fantastic that there is practically no reason for a customer not to like to engage with it at a glance. The quantity of distraction in the metaverse further reduces consumers' already short attention spans in the digital world (or metaverses). Furthermore, you must guarantee that when people first contact your product or service, they feel motivated and captivated. Then, not long after, you must optimize your design for the future and deep user involvement.

Even if you succeed in bringing consumers back time after time, you are not finished. Then you will need to come up with a design that allows seasoned users to become internal and external brand evangelists. These leaders will model appropriate behavior for everyone in the experience. They will invite everyone from outside the metaverse to enter the metaverse space.

It is not simple to create such an interesting user journey around your company's product. It necessitates an in-depth grasp of human motivation and a working knowledge of behavioral economics and human biases and heuristics coupled with the touch of huge computing technology. It demands the capacity to crawl into the skin of the users. Only then, like in great games, will you be able to generate the correct human touch. You will need to grasp both gameful design and behavioral science.

- 40 -

4

TOP WAYS TO INNOVATE
IN THE METAVERSE

The way individuals connect online is evolving, with younger populations already accustomed to purchasing and interacting virtually via social media augmented reality filters, video games, and interactive, real-time content. We are experiencing a consumer behavior transformation fueled by a virtual renaissance.

The metaverse is a promise of something new, something that merges the digital and physical worlds. Metaverse opens the door of immense opportunities and possibilities for individuals and entrepreneurs alike.

With the introduction of LiDAR 3D scanners on smartphones, the mainstreaming of virtual reality headsets, and over 7 billion gadgets able to produce high 3D experiences rapidly, businesses now have a tremendous opportunity to excel in the metaverse. They are potentially lucrative business ideas to profit from the metaverse. This chapter will talk about consumer and brand benefits that will drive the development of the metaverse today and in the future. We will share important trends that businesses can rethink and adapt to create a niche for themselves in the Metaverse space.

Why would you want to make a virtual reproduction of a Canada Goose store since you could shop for a new Canada Goose coat within an

Arctic expedition experience guided by Iditarod champion and Canada Goose ambassador Lance Mackey in the metaverse? There, you can learn firsthand about the garment's basic features and performance, buy it, and have it shipped to your real-world address. In the metaverse, you can buy a new automobile while having an adrenaline-pumping test drive on the racetrack of your choice rather than from a stationary showroom of cars. You can obtain beauty tips from a personal advisor you bring into your living room from the metaverse. Why on earth would we adopt our industrial-era version of retail as a paradigm for the future in a world where everything is possible? Advertisers, store owners, retailers, and others will have to change their minds about what a "store" is.

Eventually, virtually all of us will spend time interacting, learning, working, and relaxing in the metaverse. In contrast, some people may opt to spend nearly all of their waking hours there, considering the actual world tedious, limiting, and inefficient. The ratio between the virtual and real items we own will substantially grow as we spend more time in the metaverse. Who wants to go to two distinct digital events on the same digital weekend?

Brands will take advantage of this desire by developing an ever-expanding range of virtual goods at real-world pricing. Status symbols such as the digital house you own, the digital dress and jewelry you put on, and the digital cosmetics you use will become just as essential as physical-world purchases and assets as we spend more time in the Metaverse. Indeed, the amount of time spent in the metaverse as opposed to the physical world might be considered a status symbol in itself.

For example, Obsess creates computer-generated landscapes and experiences for big fashion and beauty companies. Ikea, for example, is already utilizing augmented reality technology in its Studio app to allow users to build their own environments. L'Oréal, the world's largest cosmetics company, has created a complete range of virtual cosmetics. Gucci has also started selling virtual clothes, unveiling the Gucci

Virtual 25 shoes, designed by Gucci creative director Alessandro Michele, and retailing for $12.99 per pair.

Each of these items represents a little step toward the metaverse, despite the limitations imposed by today's technology and protocols. Growth will be sluggish and gradual until, like with the internet, enough technology, developers, and users come together to produce a tipping point.

Smart businesses will acquire virtual real estate and pay builders to expand their brand presence and experiences, selling virtual and physical items to individuals who spend time in both realms. Laggard businesses and organizations will be trapped in the physical world, and worse, in the ghetto that the legacy internet will morph into.

Virtual Stores

As physical stores and shopping centers struggle, metaverses — or the underpinnings of such — are thriving. Stores are supposed to be sociable and entertaining, but virtual worlds play these roles more than ever due to the pandemic. Consider meeting up with a buddy in a Minecraft-like environment to chill out and shop at digital stores instead of going to a single retailer's website.

So, where do we go from here? E-sports applications and merchandise are becoming more popular, indicating a logical progression toward the metaverse. Virtual goods, for instance, which were first promoted by gamers (primarily through character skins), have subsequently expanded into the fields of fashion, real estate, art, and even pets, resulting in a $190 billion industry. Customized virtual avatars, promoted by Snapchat-owned Bitmoji, Apple's Memojis, influencer and celebrity-focused Genies, and most recently, Roblox's purchase of avatar firm Loom.ai, have found a presence beyond games such as The Sims in the previous 5 years.

On a larger scale, these developments show how the internet and the real world are rapidly converging. Metaverses will, among other things, offer the spontaneity that is frequently lacking in e-commerce encounters. Aglet, for example, a "Pokémon Go for sneakerheads" app that allows users to acquire virtual shoes while walking, promises to let consumers and companies open their own virtual retail stores in the app in the future. These are potential opportunities for brands to keep an eye on and an opportunity for tech organizations to design platforms for virtual stores.

And we believe the opposite will be true in the future. We are headed as a world for Nike and Adidas to create things in the real world and then incorporate them into games. People will create their own brands in these virtual environments later in real life.

Once the technology is in place, the economic implications are enormous since the metaverse provides users with unparalleled access and absolute immersion, thereby establishing a virtual "third space."

As a result, businesses and retailers can:

- Work in a market that is less fragmented than the internet.
- Avoid "marketplace cut" from third-party discovery or selling platforms completely.
- Allow greater cross-franchise or fan cooperation rather than separate business marketing opportunities (e.g., each business has its application or website). The metaverse's open universe enables both businesses and followers to pioneer a more interactive experience.

Big tech businesses are the most probable challengers to develop the metaverse beyond gaming platforms like Fortnite and Roblox. Directing this endeavor will take vast amounts of capital, engineering skill, and a desire for dominance. Given each company's perseverance in holding a major chunk of the online job economy, social graph, and e-commerce architecture, tech giants such as Microsoft, Meta, and Amazon, will double down on this in the nearest future.

Offering virtual items may be fashionable in 2022. Still, in the next five years, the trend will most likely shift to creating more detailed, fleshed-out virtual environments that provide an interactive shopping experience.

The First Virtual Store

The official launch of Metajuku, a shopping area in the Decentraland metaverse space, was announced by Republic Realm, a metaverse real estate development and investment business, with DRESSX being one of the first virtual-only enterprises to build a store within the area. Additionally, digital artist Hanne Zaruma has developed three NFT artworks inspired by DRESSX collections devoted to SpaceX launches.

Metajuku is a 16,000-square-foot project featuring a pedestrian-friendly open area in the heart. Metajuku has its origins in Harajuku, a Tokyo neighborhood recognized for being the epicenter of Japanese street fashion.

As stores transfer more brands online, physical-world shopping centers are sitting half-empty. Complex virtual malls being developed in the metaverse led to a new sector termed 'de-commerce.'

How to Create a Virtual Store in AR

Do you want to start your virtual store? We've prepared a virtual shopping demonstration with Unity and echoAR to get started.

- Register

If you do not already have an echoAR API key, sign up for one for free at echoAR.

- Setup

Clone the project and open the project in Unity.

Set your echoAR API key in the echoAR prefab.

Add the models from the models folder.

Add the corresponding metadata from the echoAR console's metadata folder to each model.

- Run

On Unity, press the 'Play' button.

- Notes

Use your mouse and keyboard to move around the area.

When you click on a product or model, you will be sent to the item page to replicate an add-to-cart action.

The DRESSX digital store was built with zero-gravity elements, with digital clothing hanging in the sky in zero-gravity balls.

DRESSX virtual products are available in the DRESSX digital flagship shop at coordinates 94, 21 in Decentraland.

Customizers and Configurators

With the metaverse becoming the reality of commerce, businesses must act now and incorporate new tools, concepts, and software to avoid being left behind.

Consider allowing a customer to check if a couch, desk, or table looks nice or even fits in their space before purchasing and installing it. Consider how, if it doesn't, they may make changes to assure that it does. This, and more, is achievable with Product Configuration and 3D configurator software on the metaverse.

Users may create bespoke things using a product configurator tool, which enables them to design and pick a variety of features before applying them in real-time. This removes the human element's experimentation and effort while still enabling requirements, adaptations, and processing on the manufacturer's end.

Why you Need Product Configuration

One of the key reasons to use product configuration, as mentioned above, is to present all conceivable combinations of all your items. Nevertheless, there are a number of other advantages to using this technology for your brand.

- Customer satisfaction and customization

The use of product configuration technology in the metaverse eliminates the element of surprise from virtual shopping. It offers the buyer confidence and comfort that the customized product is completed and completed correctly. They increase sales by offering consumers high-quality, immersive images that help them grasp many product possibilities. Customers may modify or pick the choices they want for a given product using a product configurator, which provides them with a unique and interesting shopping experience; in the end, everyone wins from using product configurator technology.

- Customer Interaction

Product Configuration involves the customer by including them in the process and personalizing it, resulting in a more engaged feeling and increased sales. After implementing this technology, Nike saw a 32 percent increase in sales and an 84 percent increase in virtual sales.

- Teamwork

The pandemic has altered not just how we purchase but also how we interact with colleagues. You may now use configurator software to bring your team together virtually. Website asset management, marketing, and product creation may all benefit from 3D configuration technology.

This discussion of the metaverse and a virtual environment may seem intimidating. However, product configurators may be a straightforward approach to adapt your brand to the metaverse.

Gamified Commerce

As commerce became more immersive and social, many of the enjoyable, participatory, and social aspects of shopping vanished. It did, nevertheless, open up a whole new range of other entertaining and interesting activities that may render shopping even more addicting than before – only this time from the comfort of your own home, where you can attain your win-states much more frequently.

This is when e-commerce Gamification enters the picture. Most e-commerce gamification instances have successfully increased sales and conversions by quadruple in the correct direction, and some have even assisted e-commerce sites in becoming billion-dollar corporations!

We have put up a list of fantastic e-commerce Gamification examples that will inspire intending entrepreneurs and change how we purchase.

eBay's Bidding and Feedback System

When it comes to early great gamification, few could rival eBay's potential to bring out our Core Drives. If you were only thinking about starting an e-commerce business, having a competitive bidding system, real-time feedback, and stars for leveling up that eBay offered would not seem necessary.

The exciting thing about eBay is that, unlike other e-commerce sites, buying products on eBay is more than simply a "buy" as you feel like you WON! Even though you spend 10% more than you intended to spend, you feel like you had beaten the other scumbags who were bidding against you, securing your win. This is a fantastic example of Core Drive 2: Development & Accomplishment.

Woot.com's Daily Deal System

Woot, a virtual merchant, only provides one original product per day. Limited numbers are available at a discounted price. A new product will be released when the initial product's stock has been depleted. People will look forward to the product being released, usually around midnight.

Because each product is restricted and unknown ahead of time, there are a variety of elements that impact the site's visitors. They are aware that the following thing might be wanted while yet being restricted in supply.

They are also aware that they may be unhappy with the outcome and have no interest in purchasing the product. As a result, Woot's users are enticed by the desire to learn more about what will be given and how rare the item could be.

Nike's Angry Winter Campaign

Nike introduced an online game in 2011 where participants were required to assist athletes in staying comfortable when training outside in the cold of winter. It was a part of a multi-media campaign to advertise their winter sportswear at the end of the year.

The players were given a chance to interactively aid a famous athlete they desired in "beating the weather" via a series of activities. Using the User interface, each player may control their athletic avatar (screen picture) to perform a set of actions. During these events, players may put their reflex ability to the test and win rewards for performing various tasks.

The players' abilities became more apparent as the game progressed, and the scores were tracked on a leaderboard. The top scores between December 9 and 15 were then considered for winning a two-person vacation to meet a Nike athlete.

The website offered people to purchase the new Nike winter wear worn by each athlete, indicating that this was not just for fun. It is a pretty normal competition and a good illustration of how a company might utilize an online game to promote a new product line.

Best Buy's CityVille Presence

Zynga estimates that over 230 million gamers play its games. Of these, over 71 million Facebook users play on CityVille, its most popular game. Players design structures and highways to build their virtual towns, collecting points to open up new game features.

Best Buy became the pioneer virtual retail store in CityVille. Zynga's players were able to build a local Best Buy store in their own city. Other firms could be included in the game, but they all had generic names such as "bakery" or "hardware store." Players who choose to include a

Best Buy to be visible in their virtual city indicated that they like the brand. This added reality to their virtual world experience.

Suppose a player is successful in obtaining these products. In that case, a smartphone, refrigerator, television, DSLR camera, and a Deal of the Day badge will be given with a unique decoration from Best Buy. Players might gather numerous bonuses from the brand regarding high payouts, extra points, energy, and unique items, much like in the more typical enterprises.

Creator Economy

The booming stock market and the increasing popularity of additional or side hustle are two unanticipated by-products of "working from home." We are not saying that is good or bad. Still, the present COVID-induced economic instability encourages individuals to hunt for alternative sources of income to preserve economic stability.

Even high-income workers who already live well have unexpected part-time occupations in their leisure time due to Covid allowing them to save time from the inefficient daily commute, business travels, and conferences.

One of the metaverse's main goals is to make a significant contribution to the creator economy. More paid online jobs, subscription services, and virtual retail sales will be mainstream in the nearest future. It is no surprise that the Roblox game application economy has over 10,000 artists generating big money. A woman in her mid-twenties has sold over 1.3 million virtual products on the avatar software Zepeto. The creator economy is a worldwide concern. Most businesses and organizations are working to create inclusive and equitable cultures that value people from all walks of life. This year, we are focusing on diversity, equity, and inclusion (DE&I). DE&I efforts require cross-organizational buy-in from all levels of an organization.

Zoom does not have a high table. As a result, all participants and attendees take part in a conference call as equals. In many respects, remote employment has balanced the playing field. Zoom video conferencing has removed barriers. In video conferences, we get to have more junior colleagues who would ordinarily be exempted. It allows workers to form a closer relationship with their employer as individuals when senior colleagues attend a meeting from their home while their pets run about in the background.

No one is perfect, but some love and would like to improve their appearance on Zoom. Lighting is crucial to them. In Zoom, anyone may quickly build up a chroma key background. It is a little like real estate voyeurism, because their natural surroundings reveal a lot about who they are. Individuals frequently dress in bright colors from head to hip, rather than head to toe, with work clothes on top and pajamas below.

To appear professional, individuals attempt to locate the finest background or digital wallpaper. It is common for individuals to use Zoom to expose their faces and increase their online presence to participate in greater human interaction. However, it is possible to have too much of a good thing. When a video is required on Zoom, there is nowhere to hide.

The metaverse, on the other hand, provides you freedom. You may be anybody or whatever you choose, and you can customize the texture, backdrop, and mood of your experience. Furthermore, the metaverse will provide a tremendous platform for amplifying the variety and inclusion of many viewpoints. Frankly, who cares who you are or what you do when you enter a virtual environment as your avatar?

Platforms in the metaverse can appeal to a wide range of viewers, regardless of gender, age, ethnicity, or sexual orientation. The metaverse brings individuals together to form social bonds and better understand one another without biases based on looks. During the Covid outbreak, we saw firsthand how the metaverse might minimize prejudices based on race, ethnicity, country, location, and socioeconomic position.

When people gaze about the metaverse, they see that everyone appears the same and no attachments connected. In the metaverse, there are no restrictions on creative self-expression. NFTs can also be created, and individuals can be paid only for their creative work.

The world of employment will undergo a significant upheaval. In a recent release, Meta stated that it intends to become a metaverse firm. It has amassed augmented reality and virtual reality assets to construct virtual platforms over time. The metaverse is meant to be a fun place to hang out, but it can also be a productive workstation.

Microsoft is developing the same thing, although it plans to concentrate on the corporate metaverse rather than a social platform. Many analysts believe that Meta will eventually bring people together for business, whereas Microsoft may enjoy it.

The good news is that by ripping down borders, constraints, and conventions across diverse material worlds, the metaverse might open the path for labor equality. Individuals may now choose to live outside of cities, owing to the virtual transformation, yet actively engaged in the creator economy via digital labor, regardless of where they are or how they work.

The avatar economy, which I think is a precursor to the metaverse space, where virtual items are extensively sold and exchanged on a secondary market, is already a possible tremendous boom for the online gaming business. In the actual world, income disparity has been increased by technology, trade, and financial globalization. In the metaverse, there is already a labor mismatch. Mineral mining, for instance, is nothing new in multiplayer games like "StarCraft."

Individuals in low-income nations spend their days and nights accumulating digital stuff to sell either within or outside of the game. Nevertheless, as the metaverse spreads, the value of digital labor will rise, presenting unprecedented opportunities. In theory, everybody in the metaverse might be treated equitably, and everybody seems to be at the same starting place. Although no one now rules the metaverse, it will be constructed and fine-tuned to satisfy the market's ever-changing demands. Is it possible for the metaverse to construct a distinct world?

Will existing tech behemoths continue to rule and control the metaverse, or will a new underdog hero emerge soon? Irrespective of brands' scale, creators can benefit tremendously by leveraging the range of opportunities currently available.

Increase Sales Conversion

Augmented reality and 3D features have been proved to enhance e-commerce conversion rates time and again significantly. This is possible for the metaverse. This section examines evidence from top brands, investigates why customers are so enthusiastic about 3D and AR, and assesses the financial rationale for investing in interactive technology to boost conversion.

3D in E-commerce

3D models are the most realistic way for brands to present their products online, outperforming even high-quality photos and video. However, the advantages go beyond appearance; companies make online buying an active, rather than passive, experience by providing interactive tools to customers.

Customers who can zoom, spin, and examine an item in 3D are typically more engaged, as evidenced by the research. Buyers who saw an item in 3D were 25% more inclined to buy it, according to MADE.com, while Forbes claims that 3D visuals generate 40% more conversions than 2D images.

Immersive Technology and Online Sales

ARtillery Intelligence estimates that by 2025, $58 billion in consumer purchasing will be impacted or helped by AR (up from nearly nothing in 2019). This number shows how important AR, VR, 3D technologies, and metaverse are to businesses in general and e-commerce stores in particular.

These technologies can affect every area of the sales funnel, from brand recognition at the top to product purchases at the bottom – and it is this lower-funnel behavior that has sparked some of the most well-known headlines to date.

Shopify, a Canadian e-commerce company, cites internal statistics showing up to a 250 percent boost in conversion rates when 3D & AR is presented on product pages — a figure made all the more impressive given the site's massive transaction volumes.

Overstock.com, a US-based furniture store, claimed conversion rate increases of up to 200 percent when consumers utilize 3D/AR for product visualization. At the same time, Houzz, a furniture business, recorded an 11x increase in conversions after using AR.

Immersive Technology Sales Success

In December 2020, DFS, the UK's top sofa store, provided a particularly striking piece of data. With over 120 showrooms, the business is so closely associated with its item in the UK that 'DFS' is the most widely googled phrase in the industry, even ahead of 'sofa.'

We believed metaverse, 3D, virtual reality, and augmented reality would provide a unique shopping experience. So far, the outcomes have been fantastic. Despite their brand recognition and status as a traditional bricks-and-mortar business, the firm invested in the largest web-based augmented reality deployment in January 2020, delivering visualizations for over ten thousand goods.

According to PR Newswire, the findings are impressive: consumers who engaged with the interactive technology saw a 112 percent increase in conversions compared to those who did not – and, more importantly, a 22x ROI in immersive technology.

How Immersive Technology Boosts Consumer Confidence

Even before the Covid outbreak, Google discovered that 66% of consumers wanted to use interactive technology to help them purchase, and 60% wanted to be able to see where and how an item would fit into their life. Simply defined, product visualization is a consumer issue that immersive technology can help with.

The effectiveness of AR in this domain may be boiled down to three Cs:

Consumer Confidence

Consumer confidence is boosted by the opportunity to visualize things in their homes, enabling customers to check for size, style, and fit while also reducing the possibility of organizing returns.

Convenience

Visualization removes the need to visit a real shop, eliminates the need for measurements and style samples, and reduces the possibilities of a product arriving that does not suit the buyer's expectations.

Control

AR interaction provides purchasers a better overall sense of agency, which is important for high-value, deliberate purchases. The businesses that have had the most success with AR have followed the concept of 'putting it squarely in the consumer's path,' integrating it as smoothly as possible into the consumer purchase experience. The fact that this may appear paradoxical in the buying funnel attests to the strength of augmented reality as a sales tool and customer demand for it. All these and many more prove the potential of metaverse to sales conversion.

5

VIRTUAL AVATARS

Virtual meeting rooms enabled by Spatial help teams overcome many of the challenges posed by the pandemic restrictions. Employees can connect with their team using augmented and virtual reality devices like the Oculus Quest, iOS, Android, and a simple interactive web browser. The ability to generate realistic bespoke avatars is a significant element that helps create a better meeting experience. The sensation of presence is substantially more comparable to a genuine meeting with a more accurate portrayal of each participant in the virtual environment.

We will provide you with some pointers on how to make your own avatar.

How to Create a Spatial Avatar

Making the procedure simple is an important part of providing a quality virtual meeting experience. You do not want to have to put in a lot of effort to have things set up. Virtual reality avatars are so simple to create using Spatial that anyone can achieve it in minutes. To get started, all you have to secure is a Spatial account.

- Make sure you have decent illumination and a camera or a straightforward headshot.

- The avatar may be any character with two eyes, a nose, and a mouth.
- Change the colors of your shirt and arms to your preference!

Getting Started

Begin by registering for a Spatial account. You may use related services such as Google, Microsoft, or Slack to register for an account. You may also use your email address to set up an account. After you have made your account, you will be asked to design an avatar. You can change your avatar by selecting the Edit Profile option. This may be done with your webcam or by uploading a photo of yourself from your smartphone. Make sure you get a decent, clear picture of your face while taking a picture for your VR avatar. With a neutral look on your face, look straight towards the camera. That implies there will be no grinning in the avatar photo. Do not think of it as a selfie if you are taking a photo. Rather, approach the photo as if it were a headshot for an ID photo.

A menu will also appear in your account profile; if you select Edit profile, you will be able to update or modify your avatar anywhere anytime. You can equally make modifications to your subscription, Team, uploaded content, and integrations.

- **Color and Lighting**

Another essential aspect is lighting. Make sure you are taking a picture of your Spatial avatar in a well-illuminated environment. Natural light is also preferable to artificial light when taking avatar pictures. You should also avoid using intense lights. Spatial will utilize a decent photo of the front of your face to produce a 3D bespoke virtual reality avatar that looks like you. You may then utilize the skin tone slider to alter your avatar's appearance and adjust the color of their clothes. When you are through designing your avatar, click Looks Good to exit the avatar creator. You may choose Regenerate Avatar to restart with a fresh photo if you do not like the one you previously created. It is that simple to make your virtual reality avatar. It takes only a few minutes and does not need any particular 3D modeling skills or expensive technology.

- **Customizing your Avatar**

Users like customizing their avatars to look and feel like them! We like to continue to enhance our avatar systems so that they may incorporate whatever we wish to express ourselves in virtual environments. For the time being, you can build whatever humanoid face you like, as well as a male, female, or soon, non-binary avatar body.

If you are a hand talker, you may additionally embody the avatar by employing hand tracking in your virtual reality headset to convey your full natural self. If you connect over the web, you may still emote by pressing the numbers on your keyboard corresponding to various movements or dance moves!

- **Changing Your Virtual Reality Spatial Avatar**

You may change or edit your avatar at any point! Your appearance never binds you. Simply open the Spatial account in a web browser or use the Spatial application to change the avatar. When your account is open, click Profile by hovering over your name in the top left corner of the page. You may edit your avatar's picture, adjust the skin tone, adjust the shirt color, and adjust your name from there. Creating realistic 3D avatars for team members improves the virtual reality meeting experience significantly. It seems more like a face-to-face encounter and provides a more customized experience. Creating a realistic avatar using Spatial is as simple as taking a decent photo of your face.

AI Avatars

People are more comfortable communicating with human-like entities, which puts AI avatars one step ahead of regular bots. Avatars can boost consumer happiness and sales, according to data from both the academic and corporate worlds. Newcastle University researchers placed a pair of eyes on a supermarket charity bucket. They discovered a 48 percent increase in contributions. PricewaterhouseCoopers (PwC) conducted a poll in 2018 that mirrors this conclusion. According to the report, 75% of customers want to see more human engagement in the future. This immense potential can be mainstream into the metaverse considering the rapid development of the space.

- **Potentials of AI avatars**

Brands and entrepreneurs in the entertainment industry are putting money into the market. Uneeq and AI Foundation, both Avatar businesses, raised $10 million in 2018, while Soul Machines raised $40 million in their Series B investment in January 2020. The game company Roblox purchased the digital avatar business loom.ai in December 2020.

Possible Applications of the AI Avatars in the Metaverse

- **Virtual Assistant**

Remember Clippy from Microsoft twenty years ago? Its goal was to show consumers how to use Microsoft technologies. Several virtual assistants are now available in apps and on the internet to aid their users. Individuals may converse with AI tools more comfortably and increase human-like contact with them by utilizing AI avatars as virtual assistants

A British international hotel firm has employed Amelia as a virtual assistant, according to an IPSoft case study. While it understands 90 percent of the inquiries she gets, she has learned more than 50 new procedures in only one month. According to the report, her responsibility has expanded beyond the 32 percent of the workload she presently manages.

- **Gaming**

Customized service is critical for client satisfaction in practically all businesses. One of the most common sectors where AI avatars may flourish is the gaming business. Most digital human games have been available for decades, and their visual quality and capabilities continue to improve. While games are becoming more lifelike, they may now provide you with additional alternatives depending on how you engage with them.

- **Communication**

Individuals may now design their own AI avatars using technologies like Samsung augmented reality Emoji and Apple Memoji, thanks to recent breakthroughs in mobile AI. Individuals may utilize different emojis on their digital avatars when texting to one other, and they can construct their digital avatars by shooting images.

- **Training**

Brands may use AI avatars to study and teach their employees online. This would save money on training and boost staff productivity. Walmart's employees were trained for Black Friday using computerized human avatars. TaleSpin, for instance, built Barry, an AI avatar, to help human resource teams prepare for challenging interactions. Barry pays attention to human resource staff when they announce that he will be dismissed, and he reacts accordingly. Employees may be politer in conveying challenging messages by practicing with Barry.

Popular AI avatar firms

- **Soul Machines**

This company aspires to build virtual machines that may learn and engage with the outside world the same way people can. It provides digital process automation and personalization for enterprises. According to Soul Machines, 89 percent of its clients have accomplished their objectives with its digital avatar solutions.

- **Samsung**

Samsung launched Neon, their latest AI avatar, at CES 2020. With its human-like look, Neon aspires to enhance human interaction as a virtual assistant. While Neon can display emotions, learn from experiences, and define itself as a "more autonomous" virtual entity, it pledges to safeguard your secrets. It can even teach you yoga if you so choose.

A few more firms that offer AI digital avatar services are listed below:

ObEN

Talespin

The IncLab

The AI Foundation

Uneeq etc

Facebook Avatars

Facebook Avatars are undoubtedly the newest way to transform oneself in a virtual environment without spending time playing a massively multiplayer online role-playing game or attempting to recreate the Matrix in the physical world.

Having a Facebook Avatar enables you to redefine yourself if you have become tired of the rigors of contemporary life or your physical look. OK, it will be in the shape of a cartoon Bitmoji on a site rich with the radical left and right-wing ideas, as well as inspiring postings from your aunt who does not understand current social media clichés. You will, however, be able to build an ideal version of yourself or even a disgusting replica if you so want.

Avatars on Facebook are really simple to create and utilize. Keep reading to learn how to create a Facebook avatar.

What is a Facebook Avatar, and how can I design one?

- Create or log into a Facebook account.

The first step for designing a Facebook Avatar is to enter into your Facebook account through the Android or iOS application. If you do not already have the application, you may get it from the Google Play Store or the Apple App Store.

- Click on the Facebook app menu

To reach the menu option, click the three lines that depict the menu options in the Facebook application, or swipe right a few times.

- Begin working on your Facebook Avatar.

After you land in the Avatar area, the remainder of the procedure to build your Facebook Avatar is simple. The procedure will direct you to choose your avatar's skin tone, followed by the desired haircut.

Following that, you will be able to customize your eye color, eyebrow shape, face shape, facial hair, and other features that characterize your face. You may also choose whether your avatar should be wearing glasses or lipstick.

After you have finished designing your avatar's head and face, you will be able to select the body shape and dress. Lastly, if you are a hat person, you will choose from a variety of headwear options. When you are finished, click next to have your avatar ready to use. It is that easy; there is no need to post images or allow Facebook access to your personal information.

You should have an Avatar that is a good representation of yourself; after all, you may make whatever Avatar you choose.

Metaverse Avatars

When discussing the metaverse as a single digital world, we must also consider expressing ourselves using our avatar. As a nonfungible token, you may use CryptoAvatars to build a fully customized 3D avatar representing you across the metaverse. Before we go into the technical details, let us look at why the avatar idea is important.

Our cryptocurrency wallets are already, to a certain extent, a data-driven depiction of us in the metaverse. Our wallets indicate how much money we have, which DeFi dapps we have used, what games we enjoy, and where we get our nonfungible token art. To a certain extent, wallets serve as a doorway into someone's soul.

Web domains such as .crypto by Unstoppable Domains is a method to get your wallet identified by anything that sounds like a username. CryptoAvatars and Genies are two examples of such initiatives that allow you to create your virtual avatars. These projects provide you the opportunity to create a visual representation of oneself that might be identical to you or entirely different.

A visual representation doesn't need to resemble you. We have already seen individuals adopting Avastars as a representation in the nonfungible token realm. WhaleShark, in particular, has taken it a step further by presenting his most valued Avastars figure as a visual overlay during live interviews. These avatars identify you as a certain individual in the metaverse, on the internet, without disclosing your true identity. Do you want to change your identity? Then change your wallet, which will alter your avatar, and hence your identity.

CryptoAvatars

CryptoAvatars is a curated network where artists may launch their avatars and make them available in various virtual reality Chat, Webaverse, and Somnium Space apps. Let us look at how we may use the CryptoAvatars platform to upload our 3D character designs.

Character Technical Requirements

When you are finished creating an avatar, double-check that it meets certain criteria. A total of 7,500 triangles are required for avatars to be utilized in virtual reality Chat. Make sure your avatar is fashioned like a humanoid (two arms, two legs, a body, and head) and works with Mixamo, a 3D computer graphics system software. Anyone with an Adobe license can use this program for free. To add facial actions to the avatars, you will have to employ blend shapes. Finally, the VRM file should be no more than 25MB in size.

- Begin by creating FBX file.
- Create a 3D character in Blender. Check the arms, legs, body, and head. On YouTube, there are a plethora of character-

building instructions. But take your time to learn it! It will be well worth the effort. For the time being, we are assuming you have already created something fantastic!

- When exporting from Blender, ensure the rig, mesh, and blend shapes are all included. Note that the total number of triangles is limited to 7,500.

- Select File > Export Selection > Export as FBX format (ensure Animation and Deformed Models have been chosen, choose Centimeters in Units, and use the FBX File Format: FBX 2013)

- Import FBX into Unity. Ensure Unity is installed on your computer. Use Unity version 2019.3.9f1 to design a new project.

- VRM.dev is where you can get the VRM software development kit. Make certain you purchase the Unity package! After you have finished downloading, click and drag it into Unity. There will be a VRM folder and a VRM menu item in the tool menu on top once the setup is completed.

- Within Unity, create a new folder and click and drag the FBX avatar into it. Import the texture files as well, making sure they are set to 'normal map' mode.

- Drag and drop the textures into the Main Maps 'Albedo' box by right-clicking create > Material >.

- You are now set to move the avatar about. Choose Rig and Humanoid as your Animation Type from the drop-down menu after clicking on the Mesh file. Apply, Save Scene, and now it is time to fine-tune your Rig.

- The characters' ligaments must match the right designation in this case. The left upper leg must be distinguished from the right upper leg. If you are not sure, go to Pose and then Force T-Pose.

- When you are through, Pick Mesh from the Scene menu, then go to the VRM menu option at the top, choose UniVRM from the drop-down menu, and then click Export Humanoid.

- Fill in your information, then choose Force T-Pose, Pose Freeze, and Use Experimental Export. Then save it in the same folder as the rest of your avatar files. In your project section, fresh folders will emerge.
- Remove the Mesh from the Scene menu and replace it with the Pre-fab in the Scene. It has a T-Pose straight away.
- Select Mesh > VRM > UniVRM > Export Humanoid once again. Force T-Pose, Pose Freeze, and Use Experimental Export should all be unchecked at this point. After that, export.
- You have now created a VRM file. Remember that this avatar is not entirely compatible with virtual reality Chat just yet.

Connecting with CryptoAvatars

You may now apply for your admission into the metaverse after you have designed your avatar:

- Use the pre-application form to enroll. Before accepting a creator into the space, the team must see at least one example of an avatar in action.
- On Discord, the makers of CryptoAvatars, Polygonal Mind, provide a special forum for creators. So, if you want to communicate with them easily, join their Discord server.
- They will supply you with a simple guide if you are unfamiliar with creating a nonfungible token or avatar onto the blockchain network. This comprises a Blockchain knowledge guide, a Metamask tutorial, a guide for setting up an account and uploading the avatar to the space, an Avatar Technical Guide, and Polygonal Mind's internal material on avatars.
- Polygonal Mind invites creators to contribute drawings and 3d models of their avatars. They will make sure that all avatars meet the technical specifications for the metaverse avatar standard.
- Polygonal Mind will test if the avatar fits with the virtual reality environments once the avatar is complete.

- After the avatar has been accepted, the creator must supply their personalized avatar a name, description, tags, and a 1030x1440px picture featuring his avatar. Keep in mind that the thumbnail will cut the borders.
- The designer can retain, transfer, or send the avatar after designing it.
- Because CryptoAvatars have whitelisted the creator, they can now develop new avatars and post them to the site.
- You may use your Metamask wallet to log in to Cryptoavatars.io. Design a new avatar by clicking the Create New Avatar button. CryptoAvatars will create a bespoke standard frame for your avatar. You must also supply a name, a summary, and a max of 10 tags. The VRM file should be under 25 MB in size.

It takes a lot of effort to create a metaverse avatar, but that avatar symbolizes you. It is not just a gaming character you play for a few hours, but your very own virtual rendition in a range of virtual environments. Having your customized avatar in the metaverse is highly worth it. Following this section and collaborating with CryptoAvatars will ensure that your design adheres to an open standard for avatar development. Virtual environments, certain chat systems, some games, and (hopefully) the future are all compatible with these avatars.

Microsoft Launch Avatars

Just days after Facebook was renamed to Meta to establish virtual places for both users and brands, Microsoft joined the battle to build a metaverse inside Teams. Microsoft plans to integrate Mesh, a collaboration platform for virtual experiences, into Microsoft Teams. It is part of a larger push by the business to integrate its MR and HoloLens work with conferences and video conversations that anybody may join, thanks to cartoon avatars.

With today's announcement, Microsoft and Meta appear to be on a war footing in the metaverse, especially for the future of workplace collaboration. Microsoft Mesh has long seemed like the way of the future for Microsoft Teams conferences, and it is now starting to take shape. After months of employees working from home and adapting to the new work environment, Microsoft capitalizes on initiatives such as Together Mode and other initiatives to make meetings more participatory.

In an interview with The Verge, Nicole Herskowitz, general manager of Microsoft Teams, reveals, "We got hit with meeting tiredness in the virtual environment." "It was difficult to keep focused and engaged after 50 or 60 minutes in a meeting session." Together Mode was born out of that original meeting tiredness, and Microsoft now believes that Mesh can help alleviate the cognitive burden of video conversations all day.

In a move toward the metaverse space, Microsoft Teams will gain new 3D avatars, and you will not require virtual reality gear to utilize them. These avatars may physically represent you in both 2D and 3D sessions. Therefore, if you do not want to turn on your webcam, you can have an animated representation of yourself.

It is not binary. Therefore, you can pick how you want to show up, whether it is video or an avatar, and there is a number of personalized alternatives to decide how you want to be present in a meeting. Microsoft will employ artificial intelligence to listen to your speech and then animate your avatar based on what you say. You can animate that avatar based on your verbal cues, so it seems real and like it is right there with you. Move to a more interactive 3D meeting. These cartoons will now include raising the avatar's arms or animating emoji surrounding the avatar when selecting the raise your hand option.

Microsoft sees this Mesh connectivity as most valuable in interactive environments, notably in its attempts to develop a metaverse for brands. Microsoft envisions a virtual world within Teams where users can interact and engage with friends while playing games or working on projects using Microsoft tools.

We believe the element that distinguishes how Microsoft approaches metaverse from other experiences is that it starts with the human experience. These virtual worlds will operate best with a virtual or augmented reality headset, but owing to the cartoon avatar work, they will be accessible to everybody on any gadget. So, the sensation of presence, talking to someone, having eye contact, and responding is going to be key.

Microsoft also includes translation and transcription features. Therefore, you may be able to interact in a virtual Teams room with a colleague from another country with less language barrier. Microsoft Teams plans to launch these virtual environments and avatars in the first half of 2022. The idea is to walk into an interactive space and then communicate and use Microsoft's features by the first half of next year.

Within Teams, brands will be able to create their virtual environments or metaverses. Accenture has been exploring this after building its virtual campus for staff before the Covid outbreak. During the Covid outbreak, the firm used this virtual environment to onboard new personnel, which proved quite beneficial.

Microsoft's drive for a metaverse within Teams comes only days after Facebook changed its moniker to Meta. Meta concentrates on technologies identical to Microsoft's, such as a digital avatar that embodies you in virtual worlds. In the metaverse age, Microsoft and Meta will undoubtedly compete fiercely. With its HoloLens effort and the acquisition of AltspaceVR, Microsoft has spent time investing in this field. But Microsoft and Meta are not the only ones. Many big tech companies are turning to platforms such as Spatial to provide virtual venues for events, meetings, and work collaboration.

Microsoft has many daily Teams users and incorporation into Office to make the metaverse a reality for companies. In contrast, Meta has billions of users across Facebook and Instagram to harness for its metaverse goals. The war for the digital avatars in the metaverse is just getting started.

The Potential of Metaverse Avatars

When it comes to the metaverse, two things spring to mind. When we think of the metaverse, we think of virtual worlds and virtual avatars. Most games and digital experiences now employ a proprietary avatar system. Avatar systems are available in Oculus, VRChat, Fortnite, and Rec Room. These systems have their beauty as well as their dynamics. This configuration contradicts the metaverse's stated purpose. We require better avatars if the metaverse space is an interwoven digital environment where individuals may hop from experience to experience. Avatar systems that work across platforms are starting to emerge. Wolf3D invented ReadyPlayerMe, which plans to be the metaverse's avatar system. Many games, like VRChat, already use their avatar system. Along the way, they intend to add nonfungible tokens and other functionality.

- **What Metaverse Avatars Need**

Avatars created for the metaverse must work on experience. It must be open-source, and its participants must be able to enhance it readily. Large businesses are in charge of the existing avatar systems. They have final control over who is allowed to utilize their system. Anyone may utilize Meta's Oculus Avatars to create user experiences, but there is no mechanism for consumers to add to the avatars. VRChat's avatars can be customized by users, although they are difficult to connect to other programs. A wide range of avatars should be available. Your avatar may be whatever you want in VRChat. When you look past the anime beauties, the algorithm generates a lot of unusual and imaginative avatars. There should be more options than mere cartoons or even photo-realistic humans. This is a potential investment opportunity for intending digital entrepreneurs or technology companies to benefit and create the future of metaverse.

- **Ownership**

Participants must own their avatars if the metaverse is an offshoot of our reality. A blockchain system will provide this benefit. Avatars are created and owned by the users. There will even be a marketplace where individuals can buy and sell avatars, cosmetics, and other accessories. There are certain drawbacks to doing things this way. Governance will be difficult, if not impossible, to achieve. The majority of blockchain networks and their wallets are much too complex for the typical user. The fact that the avatars are open source and available on different platforms may further contribute to a sense of ownership. It will generate a new dynamic among metaverse users if you have an avatar that feels like it belongs to you.

- **The Future**

When it comes to creating the metaverse, there is still a long way to go. Emerging technologies such as AR, VR, and blockchain are still being developed. There are still worlds to create and connections to make. There are already certain guidelines that are evolving. Meta has lately switched to OpenXR. The first step in developing a future integrated avatar system will be to standardize things.

6

PAYMENT IN THE METAVERSE

Role of Payment in the Metaverse

Payment is described as support for online payment systems, platforms, and activities. It is the legal cash and digital currency exchange, currency trading, financial services like Bitcoin and Ethereum, and other blockchain technology. Metaverse payment will be made possible by the existence of both legal and digital currencies. Based on China's present regulatory rules for digital currencies such as Bitcoin, the conflict between centralized and decentralized money will remain in the metaverse.

Payment comprises the recognition of persons and brands, the evaluation of products or services, and the agreement on transaction details to grasp the most fundamental logic of payment.

- **Recognition of Individuals and Corporations**

Payment is made with cards and mobile phones in the physical world, while authentication is done with passwords, biometric data, and other techniques. People keep their unique serial numbers on a secure carrier. We must investigate what constitutes a secure carrier in the metaverse. Integrating SE security chips to every metaverse device, like virtual reality headsets with SE security chips, turns it into a carrier carrying payments under the existing security route. However, the metaverse's unique identifying code for users and businesses has many possibilities, like the latest fire nonfungible token technology.

- **The Process of Determining Goods or Services**

In the metaverse, goods and services become digital, such as in games. If a product can alter information with easy copy, paste, and delete, and its worth fluctuates dramatically in a short period, the transaction has major flaws. This problem can be better solved with the use of blockchain technology and NFT technologies.

- **Consensus on Transaction Records**

According to the conventional online payment concept, the account owner will rule the world, and the likelihood still applies to the metaverse. If there is identity verification, the account system will have a functioning space. It has to function similarly to the present e-commerce system's role or method so that both entities are comfortable with the transaction's substance, which the blockchain network's consensus system can do.

- **Preparation for Payment Companies**

Meta announced the crypto initiative Libra in 2019. The giants were already studying the payment systems required by the metaverse before the metaverse buzz. Libra hopes to be a new decentralized blockchain network, low-volatility crypto, and smart contract system to provide a new avenue for credible financial service innovation. Libra is the keeper of a "basket of currencies" made up of international legal currencies, sometimes known as "stable currencies."

Participating institutions started to withdraw because of the multi-national compliance challenges. Therefore, Libra was rebranded Diem and focused on the US dollar stable currency. Furthermore, Meta is actively marketing the digital currency wallet concept, and its Novi division just conducted a small-scale experiment.

After being rebranded as Meta, it can securely manage payment channels and establish a strong basis for the growth of its metaverse plan with the support of its crypto project structure. Domestic enterprises have not developed preparations for bitcoin projects in advance due to governmental constraints, but there have been efforts to support virtual reality scenarios.

Alipay debuted VR Pay in 2016. The user places an order by selecting the product on the smartphone virtual reality platform or virtual reality App, confirming the purchase, entering the payment link, selecting Alipay, and clicking to complete the payment.

Finance and Payment in the Metaverse

In principle, Alipay's VR Pay is a continuation of the scheme based on Alipay's account framework. It is still a digital payment that falls within the e-commerce payment class. Furthermore, several banks are utilizing virtual reality technology to enhance the customer experience.

Many banks, like Industrial and Commercial Bank of China, Bank of China, and Hua Xia Bank, presented virtual reality equipment during the 2016 China International Finance Exhibition to give consumers a fresh financial service experience. The Guangdong branch of China Construction Bank finished the design of the "Golden Bee" maker space in 2016. Through a 6-and-a-half-minute virtual reality experience video, the Guangdong Branch of China Construction Bank and Heixia.com partnered to develop the VR experience. The potential use case of virtual reality systems in customer experience, financial transactions, scene presentation, and other areas was discussed. Guangzhou Rural Commercial Bank put up a virtual reality business hall at the 6th China (Guangzhou) International Financial Exchange Expo, where clients may explore information and do self-service purchasing.

Nevertheless, at the time, banks' understanding of virtual reality was still limited, and most employed virtual reality technology to deliver information. Therefore, it fell short of the current metaverse interoperability. Exploring how to locate situations and give services in the metaverse will become a popular issue for financial institutions in the nearest future.

Unsolved Problems

Payments in the metaverse may get more difficult in the future. For instance, consider the present game sector. The pricing of the same game varies according to the console platform, as does the division situation. Accounting needs vary depending on the platform sharing method, copyright, suppliers, and so forth.

There will be exchange rate issues if metaverse has cross-border transactions that are paid in regular legal tender. SWIFT has introduced many initiatives to increase the ease of cross-border transactions, including GPI and SWIFT Go. Furthermore, the Group of Twenty (G20) has struck a deal and introduced the "G20 Roadmap on Strengthening Cross-Border Payments," which includes development ideas to enhance the ease of global cross-border transactions clearly and concisely is supposed to benefit metaverse's development.

Furthermore, a largely unnoticed issue that Chinese authorities are presently focusing on is ethics. The financial and payment demands in the virtual world will eventually expand as the metaverse grows in popularity. The metaverse exists in parallel to the physical world, yet it is linked to it, and there are numerous options. This is the issue.

For example, suppose a woman utilizes a smart sex gadget. In that case, a hacker accesses the device, gains authorization to use the sex device, and issues a command to harm the woman severely. Will this be investigated as a case of rape? Another example is a user who acquires device rights remotely by paying a charge and giving instructions whether or not he is accused of prostitution with a woman's agreement.

Furthermore, there may be inconsistencies between digital currency and the physical, financial system in the metaverse. The digital currency in the game can be used to purchase a variety of digital products in the game environment. Once a game's impact has grown sufficiently, its game props and currency will be rooted in value with physical currency, like a rare tool or a skin valued at thousands of Renminbi. The digital currency in the game and the physical currency have an exchange rate.

The metaverse is no different. Virtual products have a specific worth if a virtual environment has enough impact and consumes enough user time. The most straightforward example is that Q coins will be able to buy buns in the future, and game coins will refuel. There is a financial oversight issue. However, a decentralized virtual currency with virtual props and impossible to monitor supervision will significantly influence the present financial system.

Need for Blockchain Payment System

Matthew Ball's metaverse framework addressed the metaverse's payment difficulty as the most difficult so far. According to him, the payment choices we have currently are so inefficient, unjust, and authoritarian. So, we may never have a metaverse we expected until we transition to a blockchain-based system, which has its own set of issues.

Transaction fees and time delays are inherent in the current traditional payment systems. Virtual environment-based payment systems are considerably more expensive and inefficient built on these payment mechanisms. Similarly, distribution networks (consoles, Apple, etc.) lock in customers and developers by imposing hefty fees on the latter and excluding payment rivals.

Because mobile is so prevalent and vital for mass-market development, existing metaverse platforms end up paying Apple and Google Play the majority of their revenue. However, their drawbacks are mostly their decentralized nature, which renders them inefficient and energy costly. For example, although Roblox's income-sharing agreement is tough for its creators, Apple takes a large blow itself. Blockchain and nonfungible tokens offer a potential fix and alternative to all of this.

Because of these flaws, practically all nonfungible token platforms save as much data as they could on centralized databases instead of the blockchain network. Nonfungible tokens rely on vulnerable "pointers" that might go offline at any time. Given this, it is unsurprising that some people consider the blockchain to be a major drawback. Do not forget that the virtual economy currently produces over $50 billion yearly and encompasses hundreds of billions of hours of use - all without using cryptocurrency or blockchain technology.

Blockchain-based payment methods for the metaverse have some promise. However, most current ones are placing the blockchain cart ahead of the digital world horse.

The recent $150,000 purchase of a CryptoPunk NFT by Visa might be the first evidence that these limited-edition digital assets are being treated seriously for commerce. Until recently, the selling of these "non-fungible" assets has been connected with a high-priced piece of art, but Visa's acquisition, although also about art, is mostly about demonstrating Visa's competence in the field of employing nonfungible tokens for commerce to firms. Indeed, Visa has a future goal, according to a study released in conjunction with the CryptoPunk purchase

Alethea AI that claims to have invented the world's pioneer "intelligent NFT," recently secured US$16 million in investment to construct a metaverse occupied with its avatars, and it is along similar lines in terms of the larger metaverse's potential, paired with the crucial function of NFTs. The talking, intelligent NFTs (iNFTs) produced by Alethea, which can conduct human-like dialogues, will populate the metaverse.

Supporters of a completely decentralized metaverse, in which nonfungible tokens play a key role in supporting the DeFi required for this meta-project to exist, convened recently in Paris for the Ethereum event EthCC. The importance of permissionless, trustless financial services with a high transaction rate for a metaverse to function effectively was discussed by key speaker Ben Lakoff, co-founder of NFT-protocol Charged Particles. The metaverse would also demand the storage and unalterability of a significant quantity of data, where blockchain technology comes into play.

Aside from the technological limitations of a space capable of supporting thousands, if not millions, of individuals online in the same virtual environment at the same time, one thing is certain: a DeFi financial design involving nonfungible tokens, which you might call the "MetaverseFi," is likely to be critical to its success.

Clearly, any major actors in the metaverse, such as Meta and Epic Games, will have to comply with the upcoming DeFi cryptocurrency laws when developing decentralized payment systems in the metaverse.

Outlier Venture, a UK blockchain VC firm, discovered that a cryptocurrency-decentralized core is essential for a metaverse's success: "It requires its own economy and native currencies, where value can be earned, spent, lent, borrowed, or invested interchangeably in both a physical and virtual world, and most importantly without the intervention of a governing system." Although the metaverse may be virtual, I think its usage of nonfungible tokens and Decentralized Finance to bring it to life is solidly grounded in reality.

7

BUILDING THE
METAVERSE EXPERIENCE

Things are moving quickly, and if you want to stay up with your users and rivals, you will have to get started right now. Here's a fast selection of resources to help you learn more about the metaverse and how you can use the underlying technology to generate value for your brand.

3D Modelling

3D modeling is crucial to building metaverse experiences. Hence why this section is important. We have provided a detailed guide to help you refresh your 3D modeling knowledge or set you on the path of learning. Either way, there are tremendous opportunities for creators to develop experiences that will shape the future of metaverse. You want to pursue 3D modeling as a job or a pastime. We will show you how to get started.

3D modeling necessitates a unique blend of technical and creative abilities. It is a career-oriented field with a lot of promise, especially in the metaverse. 3D modeling offers a variety of applications that may be useful in the virtual world, and it is a talent worth learning.

While it is a frequent notion that the entry barrier is quite high, this is not the case. In reality, even if you do not like to put in a huge amount of money, it is not difficult to get started with 3D modeling today. You are ready to go as long as you have a computer with a good processor and some form of a graphics card.

The fundamental concept behind 3D modeling is to build three-dimensional shapes that can be viewed in various ways. The ultimate result may be a static scene generated from a certain angle or a complex model that can be viewed from any aspect.

When dealing with 3D, you normally begin with a simple geometric shape (such as a cube, sphere, or cylinder) and alter it using different modifiers until it matches what you attempt to create. Of course, that is an oversimplified version; most complicated models are made up of several smaller shapes adjusted separately.

The basic procedure is changing their shapes on several layers. You may either move the entire object around (or apply many other changes, such as resizing or rotating it). Alternatively, you can divide it into its constituent parts and deal with them individually.

When working with a cube, for instance, you can alter one of its sides. You may also deal with specific vertices or simply one edge of that side (the corner points that connect edges). Using different modifiers, you may quickly apply significant changes to such shapes.

Choice of 3D Modeling Software

3D modeling was often thought to be a discipline that needed sophisticated commercial software to enter. 3ds Max, Maya, Cinema 4D, Houdini, and other prominent software packages are still used today. Blender, the only effective free software, existed back then, but it was not the Blender that most of us are familiar with now.

In terms of functionality, UI/UX, simplicity of use, and community support, Blender may easily compete with the main leaders in the industry today. Several studios are now expressly looking for Blender expertise, which was not the case a few years ago.

With that in mind, Blender is the ideal option if you do not wish to spend a huge amount of money on commercial software. It is capable of taking you as far as other common options available on the market. Blender is expected to grow in popularity in the foreseeable future as the development of the virtual space continues.

3D Modeling Hardware Requirements

Hardware Requirements

One of the most common criticisms of 3D modeling is that it needs powerful gear to get started. That is no longer the case.

Modern 3D programs such as Blender can be operated on even a subpar PC with an incorporated graphics card. When dealing with sophisticated modifiers or when your scene becomes huge, editing may take a while, but you will not be doing any of that when you initially begin.

A faster computer immediately translates to quicker rendering speeds when it comes to rendering. This implies that if you have the time to wait for your renderings to complete, you can get away with a low-powered machine. Keep in mind that the speed differential might be fairly dramatic. A computer with a powerful graphics card, such as an RTX 3070, could render a scene in seconds, but an older system may take days.

There are internet rendering farms that could help with this, but they are not free. This is a better way than investing a few thousand dollars on a modern computer.

3D Modeling for Business

Suppose you have decided to pursue 3D modeling for business purposes, such as building a metaverse experience rather than just as a creative pastime. In that case, you will want to concentrate on a few key areas. Selling unique models is a fantastic place to start. However, it is a saturated field.

You might also consider selling your renderings to individuals and brands in other formats, such as conventional art (prints or t-shirts). To summarize, 3D modelers are in high demand in the metaverse development industry.

You should research the industry and identify the essential abilities you will need to succeed. In this sense, each area of 3D modeling is distinct, and you will have to spend some time experimenting until you find what you want to achieve.

Getting Started with 3D Modeling

Join various 3D modeling platforms if you have determined you are ready to pursue 3D modeling. One of the best things about 3D modeling is that the community is well-developed. There are usually plenty of individuals willing to assist you and address any problems you could have.

CAD Modelling
Installation

We will begin with the installation of the CAD software known as AutoCAD. AutoCAD is not a free program; it costs 185 dollars a month to subscribe. It costs $1775 per year. As a result, it is a little expensive. You do, however, have a choice. If you are a beginner, Autodesk provides a free trial. But, in my perspective, it is legal if you can buy this even for a short period.

Free trial

The free trial period will last 30 days. Free trials are available for the following options.

AutoCAD WIN/MAC

Architecture toolset WIN

Electrical toolset WIN

Map 3D toolset WIN

Mechanical toolset WIN

MEP Toolset WIN

Plant 3D toolkit WIN

Raster Design toolset WIN

AutoCAD mobile app

AutoCAD web app

AutoCAD 2020 System Requirements

- Operating System: Microsoft Windows 10 (64-bit only), 8.1 (64-bit only), or Windows 7 SP1 (64-bit only)
- Processor: 2.5 GHz (3+ GHz recommended)
- Memory: 8 GB (16GB recommended)
- Disk Space: 6.0 GB
- Displ1920 x 1080 resolution with True Color

Identify the User Interface

You may now launch AutoCAD after it has been properly installed. There is a user interface with a lot of buttons and text on it. Therefore, let us have a look at what you need to understand about this.

AutoCAD is mostly used for drawing. Beginners, on the other hand, may use this to begin 3D modeling. The rationale for this is that all of the fundamental commands can be learned quickly using real-life examples. Let us have a look at what is included in these interfaces.

Drafting and Annotation Interface

- Application Button

The application button can be used for a variety of file-related operations. In addition, the application button provides access to the printing and file exporting operation options.

- Toolbar for Quick Access

The quick access toolbar has features for quick save, print, open redo, and undo.

- The Ribbon Area

The ribbon area has a variety of tools. Line drawings, modification, and editing options are all found in the ribbon area when you're using the drafting interface.

- File Tabs

In this tab, you can see which files are open and which are being worked on.

- UCS

In 3D modeling, the User Coordinate System is the most significant factor. In AutoCAD, there are two major coordinates. Both the UCS (user coordinate system) and the WCS (world coordinate system) are used. Both may be altered depending on our needs and location. We may adjust the work plane and direction using them.

- Layout Tabs

The most often used layouts in AutoCAD are model and plotting layouts. These tabs allow you to switch between printing and working layouts swiftly.

- View Cube

The view cube contains all three-dimensional viewpoints. These are the views: front, back, top, left, right, and back. You may see the applicable view side of the item by simply clicking one side. You may see and view the model by clicking the edge.

- Navigation Bar

All navigation path processes are included in this. In this area, you may observe orbit, the navigation wheel, zoom function, and motion.

- Status Bar Toggle

This is a quick overview of the most often used drafting and annotation interface. This section handles all types of tracking (object tracking), workspace switching, and snap modes. You will understand more as your knowledge grows.

3D Modeling Interface

We will use this interface to learn more about 3D modeling. Only the ribbon and its choices may be changed here.

- Ribbon Tab

In the AutoCAD platform, the ribbon tab is the most often used tab for 3D modeling. This may be used for all types of solid and surface editing. The ribbon section allows you to do modeling, mesh editing, solid editing, drawings, altering, section editing, viewing, coordinates set, and layer management.

This is a quick rundown of the user interface. Let us look at how to make a simple 3D object now.

Fundamental Steps in 3D Modelling in AutoCAD

- Step 1: Decide on your units.

This is the very first thing you should do. Since you must be aware of the units on which you will be working. Millimeters, centimeters, meters, and kilometers are examples of standard units. So, you must choose which units you are going to focus on. After that, everything is modified accordingly.

- Step 2: Analyze the Model or Drawing

Before developing a 3D model, you must first examine the drawing, reference picture, or model and generalize the final product. When you examine it, you will notice that the same pieces are utilized several times and how the object's body should look from the front, rear, sides, top, and bottom, among other things.

What should the front look like, and how can it be seen from the sides? As a result, you must be familiar with the fundamentals of drawing—observations from the first and third angles. If you have done this before, you will be able to capture them in a matter of seconds.

- Step 3: Ideation

This section requires you to consider the final item. Which method should you use to get the object? The method should have the fewest steps possible, and the object should be 100% precise and rapid. Similar sections, mirrored parts, holes, tapering, bends, linkages, and other features can be seen during the examination. These types can be altered depending on the level of intricacy.

Separate modeling and putting them together can be preferable to modeling the entire item. As a result, you may extract various types of facts into your mind during the analysis phase. Everything should begin with drawing. So, stick with that for a more effective approach.

- Step 4 Modeling

Draw the picture first, then use 3D instructions to create and finish the object, according to the drawing you gave. In 3D modeling, the essential thing is to save and retain a copy.

- Step 5 Connecting Parts

In this stage, the different modeled objects are connected to form a single object. For a better tracking procedure, you may use snap tracking in this stage.

- Step 6: Finalizing

After modeling, create a "UNION" object to link all the connections and objects together. If the pieces are in distinct files, combine them before finalizing the project. If you use AutoCAD rendering, AutoCAD provides an excellent rendering solution appropriate for modeling objects.

- Step 7 Plotting

After completing all of the steps, you will need to plot, which we refer to as printing. In AutoCAD, you may print in a variety of methods. The ideal method is outlined below.

Plotting in AutoCAD in the Easiest and Fastest Way

- Select "Visualize" tab
- Select "Model Viewports" and then "Name"
- Make a new view name in the viewport settings and then click "OK."
- Then, on the layout switching panel, "right-click" the "+" mark.
- Then, load the "New" or "Template" layout.
- Navigate to the fully loaded layout
- Go to the "Layout" panel in the loaded layout.
- Next, go to layout viewports and choose "Named"
- Select and load the stored name.
- You may show any view by drawing on the layout.

Photogrammetry

This section will walk you through the fundamental principles of the photogrammetry workflow that is required to create experiences in the metaverse. Photogrammetry is the act of getting exact measurements from images. It entails collecting a series of overlapping images of an item, structure, people, or environment and utilizing a variety of computer programs to turn them into a 3D model.

Applications of Photogrammetry

Photogrammetry is utilized in a variety of applications. We will walk you through some of the interesting applications of photogrammetry in the metaverse.

- Artists can document or transform a previous work of art, sculpture, or natural phenomenon into something new.
- Designers and engineers need to reverse design or custom-fit new pieces onto an old product.
- Photogrammetry mixed with semi-automatic 3D modeling processes can help game developers save time generating items and settings—a typical metaverse application.
- Artwork and artifacts in the sphere of cultural heritage can now be conserved indefinitely and digitally restored and repaired.
- Curators at museums can create virtual collections to entice visitors.
- Photographers now have an additional dimension with which to work.
- Companies that seek to provide a 3D printing service for their most valuable things, pets, or family members can now do this with photogrammetry.

These applications demonstrate the potential of the metaverse, and the opportunities abound for developers and brands.

Now let's delve deeper into the concept of photogrammetry and how to get started.

The Process of Photogrammetry

- Step 1: Take Images

Take a sequence of overlapping images of the thing you want to capture. For apps with low accuracy requirements, an 8-megapixel phone camera will suffice, but we suggest an 18 MP (or higher) DSLR-type camera for optimal results. The most recommended camera is a wide-angle camera as it has the least amount of lens distortion. A fish-eye lens, for instance, will not operate unless you use applications that can effectively correct it.

It is advisable to capture the images in a circle around the object. Begin with a low-angle circle, then repeat with a higher-angle circle to cover the topmost surfaces. Aim for a minimum of 50 percent overlap between every image, with 60-80 percent being optimum. Finally, take a couple more images of regions where crucial features can be found.

Take the following extra guidelines into consideration:

- Ensure that the piece has a matte surface. Transparent items are difficult to transform. 3D scanning spray or dry shampoo spray could be used to turn reflective surfaces matte.
- Many software programs struggle to deal with featureless surfaces. Surface scannability can be improved using shoe polish, sprayable chalk, painter's tape, and stone effect spray paint.
- The image's backdrop should have enough color contrast with the item. A chroma-key background or a newspaper, as long as it does not exhibit the same colors as the item, works well.
- Lighting must remain steady throughout the session, and a gloomy day is ideal.
- For a single object, 40-50 images are usually sufficient. The more images you take, the better, as long as you do not take them all from the same spot.
- The object must occupy a large percentage of the visual space.
- During the shot, be careful not to move the object.
- For every image, use a minimum depth-of-field (DOF) as possible and focus the camera precisely on the item.
- Use a tripod to prevent blurriness and for low-light situations that necessitate long exposure periods.

Based on the amount of the dataset, photogrammetry software programs might take hours or even days to deliver reliable results, even though they are continually improving. A machine with 16GB of RAM and an Nvidia CUDA-enabled GPU is required.

- Step 2: Upload

Open your preferred photogrammetry program and import the images straight into the project library. It is typically only a case of dragging and dropping. It is necessary to confirm the camera's compatibility for specific apps. They may cross-reference them with an internal database for the software to maximize its results depending on focal length, primary point, and image sensor format. A set of distortion variables referred to as a bundle adjustment are generated as a result of this.

The images will be examined for applicability to the photogrammetry procedure in the first phase of the software workflow. A green or red symbol, for instance, may show next to or on top of a picture in the library. If a large section of the photoset is declined and shooting a fresh batch is difficult, basic Photoshop manipulation might help. With white wall backgrounds, this is a regular occurrence. Creating a trash matte mask for every image helps to further differentiate the subject from the background. Refining the images may also help since the program will recognize similar characteristics across photos more easily if they are all of the same sharpness.

- Step 3: Using Photogrammetry Software to Create a 3D Model from Images

The photogrammetry program in the background handles the majority of the computational aspect of photogrammetry. However, additional functionalities may help enhance the results.

Image Matching

Many photogrammetry software packages convert the photoset into a 3D model completely automatically. On the other hand, some take Image Matching, sometimes referred to as Correspondence Search, as a distinct phase that the user must confirm. This enables changes to the photoset to be made before the more computationally demanding operations begin. The computer evaluates whether images are suitable for further processing and searches for overlapping regions in several images in this stage. It now saves how the photos will be stitched up, similar to how a 3D puzzle is put together.

Feature Extraction

This is, once again, a completely automated aspect of the photogrammetry operation in certain applications. It is possible to split this stage into various photogrammetry software applications for possible changes and iterations before proceeding. The program searches the images for traits that can be identified across numerous images in this stage. For this, some expert toolkits employ coded markers, a very precise solution that works on shiny, clear, and rather featureless surfaces. On the other hand, most tools employ the more generic Structure from Motion (SfM) method, which focuses on thick patterns on items like texts, wood grain, facial characteristics, and other designs. Edge points, lines, and corners are also essential elements. Some methods use an innovative system referred to as Shape-from-Shading to augment the data with lighting and shading signals.

In a process called Geometric Verification, they are internally validated to filter out false detections when all characteristics have been detected. The SfM engine provides a conversion that translates feature points between pictures to guarantee that the identified characteristics fall onto the same scene point. This is a sophisticated set of projective geometry-based algorithms.

Many photogrammetry applications, like COLMAP, enable users to observe the feature creation process in real-time. It is possible to halt the process in Meshroom if the user notices crucial locations where few characteristics have been discovered. Quality can be improved. By boosting keypoint sensitivity and matching ratio, adjusting presets, and converting the matching algorithm to A-KAZE or, in certain circumstances, a brute force technique.

Triangulation

In 1480, Leonardo Da Vinci invented a method for determining the painter's origin from an art piece. In this essential component of the SfM process, something occurs. The surface points' 3D coordinates are calculated using the scene graph generated from the previous phase.

The ray cloud is created by reconstructing the lines of sight from the camera to the item. The junction of the multiple beams determines the object's ultimate 3D coordinates.

After establishing global geometry with a sparse point cloud, photogrammetry software creates a depth map by analyzing the lighting and texture of the environment. This, like a woodcarver, adds all the small touches to the 3D model to bring it to life. Advanced applications employ a technique called delighting in smoothening the illuminated and darkened portions for more homogenous lighting throughout the full surface of the model. It is even feasible to reverse-calculate ambient occlusion effects and clears them away. While a genuinely illuminated model is frequently preferred for on-screen display, a delit model is best for full-color 3D printing.

The depth map is referred to as dense reconstruction. The sparse reconstruction, which laid out all visual elements discovered previously, is then integrated into a 3D mesh format like FBX, OBJ, PLY, or STL.

The process of triangulation is carried out automatically. The user may improve the image quality by changing the Track Length, Number of Neighboring Cameras, and Maximum Points parameters. Many photogrammetry systems also let you know how many triangles are in a 3D mesh model, impacting file size and post-processing time. It is important to note that changing these variables should be done with caution because they might quickly increase processing times.

Many commercial photogrammetry software packages include extra machine learning approaches to categorize identified flora, structures, and automobiles. They can sift out moving background items like animals and people and create improved shape data based on foreground outlines, reflectivity, and brightness. Using the catenary curve fitting techniques, thin objects like steel frames and power lines may be automatically generated in 3D.

- Step 4 Post-Processing

While the analytical aspect of photogrammetry is complex, it is typically the most straightforward for the user, who simply has to drop in their photos and press a few buttons. When the 3D model has been created, the actual labor begins. Photogrammetry does not produce a waterproof mesh model that is suitable for 3D print. Floating art pieces, background sound, holes, and inconsistencies are all common issues to clear up. The item will equally need to be repositioned and resized, which photogrammetry software can perform at will.

Many software programs provide built-in post-editing capabilities; if not, a good approach is to complete the required file conversions in Meshlab and the mesh cleanup, mending, remeshing, and resculpting effort MeshMixer. This software is available for business usage at no cost.

The model will be set for 3D printing or import into a CAD system after this phase is completed and the file is stored in STL format.

LiDAR

Are you familiar with LiDAR technology? How would you feel if you could wave your magic wand and instantly know how far everything is from you? This is how LiDAR works.

After reading this, you should be on your way to becoming a LiDAR hero and start applying your skill to create the metaverse experience.

Meaning of LiDAR (Light Detection and Ranging)

LiDAR is a distance technology. LiDAR devices beam light to the ground from a plane or helicopter. The signal travels to the earth and then back to the sensor. The time it takes for the signal to return to the sensor is then measured.

LiDAR calculates a distance by tracking the time it takes for a signal to return. The word LiDAR (Light Detection and Ranging) comes from this.

How LiDAR Works

LiDAR is a technology for sampling. It puts out over 160,000 signals every second. Each 1-meter pixel receives roughly 15 signals per second. This is why LiDAR point clouds have such a large number of points.

Since LiDAR technologies are managed in a platform, they are extremely accurate. For instance, vertical precision is approximately 15 cm, and horizontal precision is only about 40 cm. LiDAR devices scan the ground from side to side while an aircraft flies through the air. While some signals may fall straight down at nadir, most will travel at an angle (off-nadir). As a result, when a LiDAR system estimates elevation, it also considers angle.

The swath width of linear LiDAR is generally 3,300 feet. New technologies such as Geiger LiDAR, on the other hand, can scan widths of 16,000 feet. In comparison to traditional LiDAR, this sort of LiDAR can cover far larger footprints.

Possibilities on LiDAR

- Elevation Models

Digital Elevation Models are topographic models of the Earth's surface. You may create a DEM using solely ground returns. However, this differs from Digital Terrain Models (DTMs), which include contours.

You may create more items by utilizing a DEM. For instance, you might create:

Slope

Aspect (slope direction)

Hillshade (shaded relief considering illumination angle)

- Digital Surface Models

LiDAR, as you have learned, looks through the trees. The light ultimately hits the earth. Then we have a return to a bare Earth. However, what about the first return to the tree?

Elevations from natural and constructed surfaces are combined in a Digital Surface Model (DSM). For instance, it adds structures, tree cover, power lines, and others.

- Canopy Height Model

The real elevation of geographical objects on the ground is determined using Canopy Height Models (CHM). This form of elevation model is also known as a Normalized Digital Surface Model (nDSM).

Take the DSM, which comprises both natural and artificial characteristics such as trees and structures. Take out these heights from the naked Earth's surface (DEM). When you remove the two, you obtain a surface of elements that reflects true ground level height.

- Light Intensity

LiDAR intensity refers to the reflective percentage. Light intensity is influenced by range, incidence angle, beam, receiver, and surface material (in particular). However, light intensity is influenced by some things. When the pulse is angled further away, for instance, the return energy diminishes.

When it comes to recognizing characteristics in land use/cover, light intensity is extremely beneficial. In light intensity photographs, impervious surfaces, for instance, stand out. This is why picture categorization, such as object-based image analysis, benefits from the light intensity.

- Point Classification

The American Society for Photogrammetry and Remote Sensing (ASPRS) gives a series of classification codes to LiDAR point categorization.

Point categorization can often fall into more than one class. Ground, forest (low, medium, and high), structure, and water are examples of these classes. Vendors frequently mark these places with supplementary classes if this is the case.

LiDAR may or may not be classified by vendors. The codes are created semi-automatically by the reflected laser pulse. This LAS categorization field is not included in all manufacturers' packages. It is normally agreed upon in advance of the contract.

Components of the LiDAR system

A LiDAR has four primary components. They collaborate to provide extremely precise and practical results:

- LiDAR sensors: Sensors on the airplane scan the earth from side to side as it moves. Typically, the signals are in the green or near-infrared wavelengths.
- GPS receivers: GPS receivers monitor the airplane's height and location. These traces are critical for obtaining correct topography and elevation data.
- Inertial measurement units (IMU): IMUs track the tilt of planes as they move. Tilt is used in LiDAR technology to determine the signal's incidence angle properly.
- Data recorders: A device records all of the signal returns while LiDAR scans the surface. These data are then converted to elevation.

8

GAME ENGINES

In this chapter, we will walk you through the basics of creating games for the metaverse. We will show you how to install the engine, use the interface, and design your first game item. Below is a friendly guide to getting you started.

Unreal Engine 4

Unreal Engine 4 is a set of game production software that can create anything from 2D smartphone games to AAA console games. ARK: Survival Evolved, Tekken 7, and Kingdom Hearts III are among the games that use it.

Even for newbies, creating using Unreal Engine 4 is quite straightforward. You can build complete games with the Blueprints Visual Scripting system without writing a single line of code! You can rapidly get a model up and running when you couple it with a friendly interface.

This section is designed to assist newcomers in getting started with game development and creating games. The following are the main points that will be covered in this section:

Unreal Engine 4 Installation

The Epic Games Launcher is used to install Unreal Engine 4. Before you can get the launcher, you must first set up an account. Select the Get Unreal option in the top corner of the Unreal Engine site. You can now download the launcher for your OS after you have set up your account.

- Open the launcher after you have successfully downloaded and installed it.
- Sign in with the email address and password through which you downloaded the launcher.
- Select Install Engine in the top-left corner. You will be taken to a screen to choose the components to install after running the launcher.

Starter Content, Templates, and Feature Packs, and Engine Source are the standard options. It is best to leave these unchecked. Here's why they are valuable:

- **Starter Content**

Starter Content is a set of resources that you can use in your works for no charge. Designs and materials are included in the content. These can be used as prototype assets or in the finished game.

- **Templates and Feature Packs**

Templates provide simple features for your genre. Selecting the Side Scroller template, for instance, will result in a project that includes a character, simple action, and a fixed plane camera.

- **Engine Source**

Epic offers access to the engine's source code, allowing anybody to modify it. If you wish to include custom functions in the editor, you can alter the source code.

Different platforms are provided as you navigate down the list. If you do not intend to build for a particular platform, you can turn it off after making your selections and selecting Install. The engine will show in your collection once the installation is done. It is now time to start working on your project.

Designing a Project

To access the Project Browser, select one of the Launch options. Select the New Project option when it appears. Select the Blueprint option from the drop-down menu. If you are starting from scratch, instead, use the Blank template.

- **Target Hardware**

Selecting Smartphone/Tablet as the intended hardware will turn off several post-processing elements. This will allow you to utilize the mouse as a touch-input device. This should be set to Desktop/Console.

- **Graphical Target**

When you select Scalable 3D or 2D as your graphical target, several comment effects will be disabled. This should be set to Maximum Quality.

- **Starter Content**

This option can be enabled to include Starter Content. Set this to No Starter Content just for simplicity.

Lastly, there is an area where you can enter the location of the project folder and its name. By selecting the three dots at the end of the Folder field, you may alter the location of the project folder. You need not panic if you wish to alter the title afterward; the project name does not reflect the game's title. For example, choose the text in the name section and enter BananaTurntable. Finally, select Create Project from the drop-down menu.

Navigating the User Interface

The editor will open after you have finished creating the project. The editor is divided into several panels:

- **Content Browser**

This panel shows all of the project files in the Content Browser. Create folders and arrange your files with this tool. You can use the search bar or the filters to look for your files.

- **Modes**

This panel allows you to switch between several tools, like the Landscape and Foliage tools. The standard tool is the Place Tool. It enables you to include a variety of items in your level, like lights and cameras.

- **World Outliner**

All the items in the present level are displayed in the World Outliner. You can categorize the things on the list by placing them in folders. There is also the option to search and filter by type.

- **Details**

The features of any item you choose will be displayed here. This panel is where you can change the item's settings. The changes you make will only affect that object. If you have two spheres and modify the size of one of them, you will only influence that sphere.

- **Toolbar**

This section contains a range of functionalities. Play is the one you will use the most.

- **Viewport**

This is the view of your level. By holding down the right-click button and dragging the mouse, you can have a look around. Hold right-click and use the WASD keys to move.

Importing Asset

In our BananaTurntable example, what good is a turntable if there is nothing to show on it? This banana model can be downloaded. You could also use your own model. You must import all files before Unreal can use them.

- Go to the Content Browser and select Import from the drop-down menu.
- Find the folder containing Banana Model.fbx and Banana Texture.jpg through the file browser. Drag and drop the files onto the desktop, then click Open.
- Unreal will offer you several alternatives for importing the.fbx file. Because you will be producing your own material, ensure that Import Materials is unchecked. The other options can be left alone.
- Select Import. Your Content Browser will now display the two files.
- Whenever you import your file, it is not stored in the project until you expressly tell it. By right-clicking the file and choosing Save, you may save it. You can also pick File\Save All to save all files simultaneously. Make sure to save frequently!

Models are referred to as meshes in Unreal. It is time to put our banana into the level since we have a mesh for it.

Incorporating Meshes into the Level

Left-click and move your object Model from the Content Browser into the Viewport to apply a mesh to the level. The mesh will be placed by releasing the left click. This enables you to spice up the level because it is looking a little boring right now. A level's objects could be dragged, turned, and resized. W, E, and R are the keyboard shortcuts for these functions.

Materials

You will need to make a material to give your object some color and feel. The surface appearance of something is determined by its material. A material explains four things at its most fundamental level:

- **Base Color**

This is the color or texture of a surface. It is used to give an object color diversity and detail.

- **Metallic**

The degree to which a surface resembles metal. A pure metal will often have the highest Metallic rating, while cloth material will have zero.

- **Specular**

Non-metallic surfaces' texture is controlled by specular. Ceramic, for instance, has a high Specular index, although clay does not.

- **Roughness**

A surface with the highest level of roughness will ordinarily have no shininess. It is used for surfaces like rock and wood.

Creating a Material

Navigate to your Content Browser and select the green Add New option to create a new material. A menu with a set of assets that you can generate will come up. To get started, go to Material. For our banana example, name the material Banana Material and then double-click the file to access it in the material editor.

The Material Editor

The material editor is divided into five sections:

- **Graph**

This panel contains all of your nodes, as well as the Result node. Pan by holding down the right-click button and dragging the mouse. By sliding the mouse wheel, you may zoom in.

- **Details**

The attributes of any node you pick will be shown here. If no node is specified, the panel will display the attributes of the material instead.

- **Viewport**

This object has a preview mesh that will be used to display the material. Hold down the left-click and move the mouse to rotate the camera. By moving the mouse wheel, you may zoom in.

- **Palette**

This is a list of all the nodes that your material has access to.

Meaning of Node

Before creating the material, you must first understand the objects utilized to create it: nodes. The bulk of the material is made up of nodes. There are many different sorts of nodes, each with its own set of capabilities.

Inputs and outputs, indicated by a circle with an arrow, are possible for nodes. The inputs would be on the left and the outputs on the right. The Result node is a unique node found in materials. All of your nodes will finally end here. The final material will be determined by whatever you plug into this node.

Adding Texture

A texture is used to provide color and detail to a model. A texture is nothing more than a two-dimensional image. They are usually projected onto 3D objects to add color and detail.

For our example, the Banana Texture.jpg will be used to texture the banana. You can use a texture in the material by using the TextureSample node. To find TextureSample:

- Go to the Palette panel and check for it. By holding down left-click and sliding the node, you can add it to the graph. Ensure the TextureSample node is selected before selecting a texture.

- Go to your Details panel and select Texture from the drop-down menu on the right. All of the textures in your work will be listed in the menu that appears.
- Choose the appropriate texture file from the drop-down menu.
- You must insert the texture into the Result node to see it on the preview mesh.
- Hold down left-click on the TextureSample node's white output pin. Then slide it to the Result node's Base Color input pin.
- To see the texture on the preview mesh, return to the Viewport.
- Rotate it to examine the additional details (by holding down the left mouse button and sliding).
- Select Apply from the Toolbar to modify the material, then leave the Materials editor — you are set.

Blueprints

Even though your object is beautiful, it would be even more so by using Blueprints. It is simple to make one. A Blueprint is a representation of a 'thing' in its most basic form. Blueprints enable you to give your objects unique features. The object could be tangible (such as a turntable) or abstract (like a healthcare system).

Do you want to build a moving car? Make a blueprint for your project. What about a pig that can fly? What about a kitty that explodes when it collides with something? Make use of blueprints. Blueprints, similar to materials, use a node-based framework. This implies you only have to create nodes and connect them; no coding is required!

Note that you can utilize C++ alternatively if you like to write code. Blueprints are simple to use, although they are slower than C++ code. If you have to use something computationally intensive, such as an advanced algorithm, C++ is the way to go.

Even if you like C++, there are times when Blueprints are a better option. The following are some of the advantages of Blueprints:

- Blueprints are, on average, faster to develop than C++.

- It is simple to organize. You can categorize the nodes into sections like functions and graphs.
- Because of its visual and creative nature, enhancing the Blueprint is simple even when working with non-programmers.
- Using Blueprints to design your things is a smart idea. Whenever you desire extra performance, change them to C++.

Creating a Blueprint

- Select Add New from the Content Browser. Select Blueprint Class from the drop-down menu.
- You will be presented with a window asking you to choose a parent class. The Blueprint will inherit all variables, operations, and elements from your parent class. Take a moment to read about the details of each class.
- Note that the Pawn and Character classes are also Actors because they can be placed and spawned. For our example, because a turntable will only be in one place, the Actor class is the best choice. The actor is selected, and the resultant file is named Banana Blueprint.
- Finally, open your project Blueprint by double-clicking it. If a window such as this comes up, select Open Full Blueprint Editor:

The Blueprint Editor

To begin, ensure the Event Graph tab in the Blueprint editor is selected. There are a few primary panels in the Blueprint editor:

- **Components**

This section includes a list of the currently installed components.

- **My Blueprint**

This is where you will keep track of your graphs, functions, and variables.

- **Details**

The features of the currently selected object will be displayed.

- **Graph**

The real fun begins here. This is where you will put all of your nodes and logic. Pan by holding down the right-click button and dragging the mouse. By sliding the mouse wheel, you may zoom in.

- **Viewport**

Any parts with a visual element will be shown in the viewport. Using the same tools as the Viewport in the main editor, you may navigate and explore.

Unity

Unity is an excellent prototype tool for everything from games to immersive experiences. With our practical guide, you can begin to create experiences in the metaverse even as a beginner. You can work with Unity whether you are a hobbyist, unity developer, 3d modeler, or graphic artist. In this section, we will go over everything you need to know to get started with Unity.

This section is for anyone who has never created with Unity before. But we strongly advise that you review your programming or web design/development knowledge. After reading this chapter, you should understand the engine and the essential functionality and code to create game and metaverse experiences.

Let's get started

Unity is a technology with the fewest perspectives. It comes with a very basic product out of the box. Still, it is extremely flexible, well-documented, and extensible, allowing you to create almost any type of game you can imagine.

Escape from Tarkov (FPS), Monument Valley (Puzzler), and This War of Mine (Strategy / Survival) are just a few of the incredibly successful

Unity games. Unity is an excellent place to develop fully functioning interactive prototypes for UX studies because it is essentially an engine with a lot of physics, animation, and real-time 3d modeling. Unity has full virtual and augmented reality capabilities, making it an excellent tool for customers to explore design, automation, and simulations.

Unity Editor Window

The editor window is divided into several components. We will only touch on this quickly because we will be referring to it frequently throughout this section.

- Scene View

This view enables you to move and put GameObjects in the scene.

- Game View

This shows how the player will perceive the scene from the perspective of the camera.

- Inspector

Displays information about the scene's selected GameObject.

- Asset / Project

Prefabs, textures, models, scripts, and other assets are saved here.

- Hierarchy

Allows GameObjects to be nested and structured inside the scene.

Now we are ready to get started

Unity Game Objects

GameObjects are the fundamental building blocks of the Unity games engine. It is almost obvious from the name. In Unity, whatever you put in a scene should be contained in a 'game object.' If you are familiar with web design, you can think of GameObjects as <div> elements.

Containers that are boring yet can be easily extended to include complicated functionality or graphics.

To emphasize this point, I have taken it straight from the Unity editor window. Everything is a GameObject, including particle effects, cameras, players, UI elements, and so on.

Making Hierarchy

A GameObject, similar to a <div> in web programming, is a container. You can nest games objects to design different and desired layouts or abstractions, much as you can nest <div>s to create diverse and desired layouts or abstractions. We will offer a few examples of how the logic behind nested game objects is similar to web development.

Clutter and Efficiency

You have a lot of identical pieces that can be dynamically created on the go in response to user input, and you want to have them organized.

- Unity Translation

You are making a Minecraft clone, and there are a lot of blocks in the scene; for performance purposes, you have to add and delete 'chunks' of blocks. As a result, they should be parented to a vacant GameObject for every chunk, as erasing the chunk parent deletes all the children blocks.

Positioning

- Web analogy

You would like the content to be positioned 'relative' to the container rather than the web page.

- Unity Translation

You have constructed a swarm of helpful drones that hover about the player. You will prefer not to write code to command them to run after the player. Therefore, you make them children of the player game object alternatively.

Components of Unity

The Actor Component Model

GameObjects are not particularly useful on their own; as we have seen, they are essentially containers. Components developed in either C# or Javascript are required to add a feature to them. Unity is based on the Actor Component model, where GameObjects are the actors and Components are the scripts.

Suppose you have ever created a web application. In that case, you are probably aware of the concept of generating tiny reusable components like buttons, form elements, and flexible layouts with several directives and adjustable characteristics and then putting these small pieces together to make larger web pages.

The degree of reusability and fully defined communication pathways between pieces are two major advantages of this technique. Similarly, with game creation, we aim to keep the danger of unexpected consequences to a minimum. If you are not careful, little errors can quickly spiral out of control and become extremely hard to debug. As a result, it is crucial to design minimal, dependable, and reusable components.

Key Built-in Components

- MeshFilter

This assigns materials to a GameObject based on a 3D mesh.

- MeshRender

This component lets you give materials to a 3D mesh.

- [Box | Mesh] Collider

This allows GameObject detection during collisions.

- Rigidbody

This allows for real physics simulation to act on GameObjects using 3d Meshes and trigger detection events on box colliders.

- Light

This component illuminates some parts of your scene.

- Camera

This property specifies the player viewport that will be linked to a GameObject.

There are many more, but these are the most important to get acquainted with. One suggestion is that you can get all of the documentation for these through the unity guide and scripting guide, which you can access from anywhere.

Making Custom Components

The built-in components mostly handle physics and aesthetics, but to truly create a game, you will have to take user input and change both conventional components and GameObjects.

Go into the chosen GameObject > Add Component > put the name of the new component in the search field > new script (c#) to begin building components. We would suggest that you use Javascript in Unity as a general rule. It has not been updated with all of the new features in ES6, and most of the more powerful features rely on C# code converted to Javascript.

Structure of a MonoBehavior

Important Functions

This comprises all components inherited from the MonoBehavior Class. It includes several common techniques, the most notable of which are:

- Void Start ()

This is called when an object containing the script is created in the scene. This comes in handy if we need to run some initialization code, such as setting a player's equipment once they enter a game.

- Void Update ()

This is where most of the user input code will go, altering various parameters like the player's movement in the scene.

Inspector Variables

We frequently strive to make components as adaptable as possible. For instance, every weapon may have varied damage, rate of fire and so on. While all weapons are the same, we might want to construct multiple varieties easily using the Unity editor.

When developing a UI component that detects user mouse actions and places a cursor in the viewport, this is another clear scenario where we might like to accomplish this. Here we might like to adjust the cursor's responsiveness to actions (if the user was using a joystick or gamepad vs a computer mouse). As a result, making these variables simple to modify both in edit mode and during execution makes a lot of sense.

During execution or modification mode, variables in the inspector window could be altered at any moment. Changes made in the middle of a run would not be permanent. We can readily accomplish this by defining them as public variables in the component's body.

Transformations

All GameObjects contain a transformed feature that allows you to do numerous helpful transformations on the current game object. The procedures above are straightforward; remember that we refer to the GameObject that holds this specific instance of the component with lowercase GameObject.

Using local [Position, Rotation] instead of the global position/rotation of an item is a great practice generally. Because the local space axis is orientated and focused on the parent object instead of the global origin and x,y,z directions, it is generally easier to move objects logically.

Creating New GameObjects

You may wish to create GameObjects on the go because they are essentially everything in your scene. For instance, if the player has a projectile launcher, you may have to build projectiles on the go that have their own contained logic for flight, damage, and so on.

To begin, we must define the term "prefab." Simply slide any GameObject from the scene hierarchy into the assets folder to make them. This simply saves a copy of the item we just had in our scene, along with all of its settings. We may assign these prefab parts to inspector variables (as we discussed before) on any component in the scene, allowing us to build new GameObjects as described by the prefab at any moment.

The prefab may then be 'instantiated' and moved to the desired area in the scene, along with the relevant parent relationships.

Raycasting

You might well have come across this when people compare 'physics-based and 'ray-based FPS games. Raycasting is similar to a laser pointer that returns a 'hit' and feeds back the object's data whenever it contacts a 'collider' or 'rigid body.'

There are two circumstances in which this is useful (and there are certainly many more). If you were creating a munition for a game, you could use raycasting to identify hits and even customize the ray's length such that melee weapons only 'hit' at close ranges. Generate a ray from the mouse pointer to a location in three-dimensional space, for example, if you want the participants to be able to pick units in a strategy game using their mouse.

The important thing to remember is that the ScreenPointToRay transformation must cast a ray in the direction the mouse is pointing in the 3d world. The purpose of this is that the camera renders a 3d space as a 2d viewport on the laptop screen, which necessitates projection to return to 3d.

Collision Detection

Earlier, we stated the Collider and Rigidbody components that can be applied to an object. The principle of collisions is that an object should have a rigid body while the other should have a collider (or both have both components). When utilizing raycasting, keep in mind that rays would only collide with things that have collider components.

We may utilize the OnCollisionEnter, OnCollisionStay, and OnCollisionExit procedures to respond to collisions once they have been established within any custom component associated with the object. Once we have the collision info, we can have the GameObject responsive and utilize what we learned before to interact with components connected to it.

One thing to keep in mind is that rigid-bodies offer physics for objects, like gravity, so if you like to disable this, make sure its kinematic is off.

CONCLUSION

The big tech corporations are heading straight into the metaverse. The computational capacity to expand virtual reality to a vast scale is becoming available. Cryptocurrencies and non-fungible tokens (NFTs) make it simpler to acquire and sell items inside the metaverse, allowing for new business options. However, more significantly, these transferable tokens will allow you to move your virtual identity and products between multiple metaverse environments in the future. This is where the metaverse actually becomes "meta," and you may jump between levels as smoothly as in sci-fi books like Snow Crash and Ready Player One.

Games are a pivotal step. However, the metaverse encompasses much more when viewed through the lens of Web3.0. Many creators will develop enterprises around delivering goods and services for the metaverse from artists to fashion brands. Conferences, education, and healthcare are all possibilities on the more business-oriented side.

Every organization, in general, is expected to have a metaverse presence. Today, every business has a two-dimensional website. There will be a 3D version of that in the metaverse space. Hundreds of businesses, from seed-stage entrepreneurs to tech behemoths, have already established themselves in the metaverse environment.

Interactive meetings and training are two examples of metaverse activities that largely rely on virtual reality gear. Before we utilize glasses, we will use our phones to experience augmented reality in diverse ways, such as trying on shoes before buying them or trying cosmetics. The most significant risk for investors is determining whether firms truly understand how to create a fascinating metaverse that individuals would like to engage with.

A battle is building about whether the metaverse will be dominated by a single firm, such as Meta, or a group of companies working together. This, we believe, is the fight that will rage for the next several years. We believe the metaverse will explode exponentially when we can truly co-create and meet individuals worldwide while working on different projects.

- 115 -

A MESSAGE FROM THE AUTHOR,

AS INDEPENDENT AUTHORS IT'S REALLY DIFFICULT TO GET REVIEWS.

THEREFORE, I'D REALLY APPRECIATE IF YOU PLEASE DO LEAVE A REVIEW OF THIS BOOK ON THE PLATFORM WHERE YOU BOUGHT IT.

MANY THANKS.